PEACE, LOVE AND HEALING

NEW TEACHINGS FROM

LORD JESUS THE CHRIST

Received by

Mikaelah Cordeo, Ph.D.

Ascended Master Messenger

Peace, Love and Healing

ISBN: 0982781814

ISBN-13: 978-0982781814

For permissions, write the publisher below:

Golden Rose Publishing
P.O. Box 810
Mount Shasta, CA 96067

email: mcordeo1@gmail.com
website: www.mcordeo.4t.com

Printed in the United States of America

Acknowledgements

I wish to thank all the Ascended Masters, Angels and Divine Beings who have supported me with their love, their wisdom, their guidance and protection during my own personal journey of transformation and Ascension, each one giving me gifts beyond measure. I thank especially, Lord Jesus, Mother Mary, Quan Yin, Goddess Isis, Mother/Father God, the Dali Lama, Gautama Buddha, Sai Baba, St. Germain, Lord Sananda, Lord Sunanda, Sanat Kumara, Commander Ashtar and Archangel Michael.

And I thank the many teachers I have been blessed to call my friends, without whose help, I cannot imagine the difficulties I'd have had to face alone. I especially thank Kathryn Shanti Ariel, Ashalyn, Luminara Ashtar Athena, Michael Buckley, Jim Calhoun, Joanna Cherry, Heather Cronrath, Thea Hartman, Carolyn Hedger, Pat Henshaw, Richard Hergenrether, Shahan Jon, Aurelia Louise Jones, Kristin Kline, Zahn LaScot, Karen McArdle, Mary Clarice McChrist, Lynn Rogers, Arian Sarris, Barbara J. Semple, Jean Snow, Shambala Songstar, William Star, Petey Stevens, Sophia Tarila, Intz Walker, to name a few, and to all the members of my family who, whether providing support or seeming resistance, were tremendous guides on my journey.

And I thank all those who were seeming students and clients along the way. Each one has been a mirror and a significant part of this journey as well.

And finally I thank my blessed cats, Donatello, Jade and Celestialah, who have poured forth, love, healing and support throughout this journey.

Author's Note

As I transcribed this message in communion with Lord Jesus, I was moved to include various Biblical scriptures. This was a clearing and a healing process for me and I know that it can serve others as well. So however personal to me it might seem, know that there is a loving message and deep healing for you as well.

In the beginning, I had tremendous difficulty with negative planetary influences as I sat to receive Jesus' messages. At one point I was ready to drop the project entirely until Jesus explained that this was the same field of planetary negativity that he had to contend with during his liftetime. Somehow, this made a difference and the entire difficulty disappeared, not to return. If you experience this, please join your prayers for healing and transformation for the planet. We are all needed in this final clearing.

For some there may still be lingering issues with organized religion and the Bible. Please use the tools of healing and transformation to clear these issues if you notice them as you read.

For myself, as I am finalizing this book, I see so many things in the way Jesus handled the introduction of so many topics by starting exactly where I was in the moment. He effortlessly turned my lessons into that which serves everyone and at the same time drew us quickly deeper into the depths of Love and Wisdom, Peace and Healing, and allowed us to touch the luminous and exquisite nature of universal consciousness.

I want to encourage you to take lots of time with each concept as you go through a chapter. As a dear friend once commented when she was teaching me how to play a duet, "It's not a race."

You can read this book straight through, but you will only be skimming the surface. Allow yourself the privilege of aligning with the blessing of Jesus' presence. There is much that can be received in the time of meditation and assimilation. It will be unique for each one. Experiment, explore, receive all the blessings.

See the **Tools for Transformation** section at the back for a summary of simple ways to clear and transmute. As well, the suggested Bibliography lists a number of other books with more detailed descriptions of various processes that are significant to the journey of Transformation and Ascension.

The Appendix also offers a list of links to text, audio and videos that offer more expanded information on many of the topics.

Preface: Jesus Begins

Blessed One,

I Am Jesus. It is my wish that these, my messages, go out to the world. I ask you in this way to add this section to that which has gone before. We begin with a commentary on the goodness of mankind. The term "mankind" already sets the intention. Man is kind. Kind is the term describing the nature of man.

I will say unto all who read these words, Acknowledge your own true nature. You are good/God in form. Yes, it may indeed seem that there is some inherent weakness in each man and woman, and yet I say unto you, it is your true nature that has chosen this battle. You have desired to test the strength of your goodness through testing it within yourself. That which appears to be an external negativity is in fact a reflection of mankind's internal battle, testing constantly his or her personal integrity.

And those actions, which on the surface might appear most wrong, are sometimes the very success of the internal battle.

So, humanity has tested itself. This phase of self-testing, self-challenging is over. It is no longer necessary to explore this question over and over in multiple ways.

We invite all to surrender to Peace. Allow Peace within to begin its rule. As Peace permeates your heart and mind, we refer your thoughts to the words of an old song:

> *"Peace will guide the planets,*
> *and Love will steer the stars."*

Introduction:

Dear Readers,

As I am reading these pages over and over in the final editing phase, I find there are so many more things I want to tell you. Part of what I hope for each of you is to get to know Jesus a little better, more personally, through these words and exercises, but also through your own unique experiences as you process your own memories and healing.

Take the time to sit in meditation with his presence. Let this time be sacred and individual, just for you. As much as each chapter seems to start with my issues in the moment, he has designed these words and these books to create a unique and personal experience for each one who reads it or shares it in their daily activities.

Allow the Love, the Wisdom and the Graces that he brings to touch your body, your feelings, your mind and your spirit.

It is my intention and my heart-felt wish for each of you to receive the maximum benefit from these teachings.

May the tools be of daily benefit to you. May the wisdom take you deeper into your spiritual growth; may you feel that Jesus is a personal friend and ever-present help; and may you each be ever more aligned with your Beloved I Am Presence that is the essence of the Ascension process.

Blessings to all,

Mikaelah Cordeo

Table of Contents

Book Three

HEALING

Appendices

Exercises

BOOK ONE

PEACE

BOOK TWO

LOVE

BOOK THREE

HEALING

BOOK ONE

PEACE

Chapter 1

The Quality of Peace

Blessed and Beloved One,

I Am with you now. I Am the One you know as Jesus the Christ. I Am One with the Father and One with the Mother, as you and I are also One in the fields of everlasting Love and Light.

We would speak to you today of Peace. Peace is a Divine quality of God which is increasing in resonance during this Time of Transition on Earth. Soon the new standard level of Peace will be reached, and it will be an everyday experience to feel and know an ever-expanding Peace within yourself and in all Life surrounding you.

Many have been praying for Peace, calling for Peace, but not necessarily knowing the details of what to expect. Peace is more than an absence of war, or fighting, or simply deep quiet. Peace is an active principle. It is a resonating frequency, which permeates each cell and atom of your being and all Life on Earth. When the percentage of Peace increases on Earth there are certain definite consequences.

Peace is an Active Principle.

Peace in your heart and mind helps you to feel safe and allows your consciousness to expand and open. When this opening occurs, the little dark places that might have been tightly hidden are revealed. Those qualities of habit or thought that formerly could reside in the dark recesses of the mind cannot remain. They must come up and out. Thus, you

3

are observing behaviors in others which are uncomfortable at best and dangerous and deadly at worst. This is the reason that this Divine Quality of Peace is being increased very gradually during this Time of Transition.

Each person is being given the chance to look at what thoughts, ideas and behaviors they have been harboring. It is a chance to look deeply at oneself and to clear, cleanse and heal that which can no longer remain hidden and buried.

Not everyone has explored the esoteric tools of the New Age practitioners such as the use of the *Violet Flame*[1] to transmute negativity. But everyone has a conscience, and all know the difference between right and wrong, between that which is loving and uplifting and that which is hateful and degrading. ,

Each person who chooses that which is "good" feels the warmth of love which expands and fills their hearts. Those that act against what they know within themselves to be "right" feel a lessening of light and a closing down of their heart.

Many years ago, there was a story of the warm fuzzies and the cold pricklies. The basic idea was that there was an endless supply of warm fuzzies and it felt wonderful to receive them and to share them with others. Somehow the idea appeared that there might not be enough to go around, but that one could substitute the cold pricklies instead. These did not feel at all good, but would also fill up the empty places within one. After a while, very few remembered that there had always been enough warm fuzzies to go around and how it felt to be happy all the time.

---

1   *Violet Flame is 7th Ray energy, which holds the Divine Qualities of freedom, forgiveness and the transmutaion of negativity. Violet is the highest frequency of the visible spectrum. More information about words or phrases in bold/italic can be found in the glossary and other links available at the book website: **www.cordeobooks.wordpress.com***

4

It is time now to understand that the cold prickly thoughts, feelings and behaviors cannot live in these new vibrations. And the warm fuzzies are still in unlimited supply and can be shared freely. They will fill up any places that feel empty, now that the cold pricklies have been revealed to be worthless and are being cleaned out.

It is the Divine qualities, the Virtues, that are the warm fuzzies – Kindness, Forgiveness, Gratitude, Sharing, and so on. And everyone is well aware of these choices.

As the qualities of Peace open and expand the heart, fill the expanded spaces with that which is loving, joyful and healthy.

Look in the mirror and honor and love what you see. Focus not on the wrinkles, the spots, the nose that don't fit your image of perfection. Ignore the weight that is too much or too little. Rather, look into your eyes and see the soul within that was created to be unique and wonderful with a specific array of gifts and talents that was exactly what was needed to add to the whole.

After you learn to see the gift that you are to the world, you can remember to see the gift that each other one is, as well. Choose to share from the endless supply of warm thoughts and fuzzy feelings and loving words and actions, and let warmth and love fill the spaces that are expanding within you. The darker, denser, colder pricklies will not, cannot, fill these spaces.

It would be a very good idea to spend time every day, noticing the little bits of negativity that are floating through your consciousness. 'She's too fat.' 'He's old and forgetful.' 'The kittens are wrecking the house.' 'I'm tired of being the one to do all the work.' On and on the comments come. Each one is not "too bad" but they add up to a stream of negativity that drags your energy and your life force down.

It is good to remember that you are not these thoughts. In fact, these small judgments do not enhance your life in any way. There is no protection or safety inherent in such negative judgments. They serve no higher purpose. In fact, many are not even your thoughts, merely random energy floating around the house, or the yard, or at the mall.

Take a moment several times a day, and ask the angels to assist you in clearing your energy field and the space around you of these negative thought forms. You might imagine a pillar of *violet flame* in front of you and quickly step into it for a quick clearing.

You may ask the angels to send violet flame throughout your home, office, school or whatever space you are occupying to clear and transmute any and all negativity.

In this way you are assisting in both personal and planetary cleanup. Spend a moment sending out a positive message or two. 'It's a beautiful day.' 'It's lovely to see you.' 'You are looking particularly happy today.' 'The sky is filled with glory, just look at it!'

What if everyone who entered your home was touched by such loving thoughts? You can create this if you choose.

I Am Jesus, with you Now and Always.

Chapter 2

What About Terrorism?

Certainly, terrorism is something that has been brought to everyone's attention these days. How can we protect ourselves? How can we make sure that terrorists don't have a chance to hurt anyone?

First of all, it is best to be aware that terrorists are human beings with thoughts and feelings just like everyone else. Some of them have had deeply painful experiences that they are attempting to deal with. Others have been brainwashed to believe that only acts of terrorism, cruelty, pain and death will bring attention to the depth of the problems that have been ignored.

It is also important to acknowledge that we have been ignoring some people who have been in terrible pain. Perhaps they have been on the other side of the world and easy to ignore in the past. Perhaps they have chosen an incredibly frightening way to bring their pain and suffering to our attention.

Are we ready to acknowledge that our choices and behaviors have led to this problem? Are we ready to do something besides lash out and try to hurt in return? When a problem has reached this level of difficulty, there are no easy answers. But each of us has a choice in how we respond to pain and suffering.

If a small child is acting out, a caring parent does more than just try to stop the behavior. They listen with both their ears and their hearts to what the child is trying to say.

They pay attention to the unspoken as well as the spoken messages. They may even take themselves and the child for counseling to find a solution that leads to healthy behavior and more joy for everyone.

When individuals or groups lash out with guns or bombs or other weapons, it is very frightening. When people are injured or killed and property is damaged, it hurts us very much. Are we ready yet to choose to create healthy environments, both at home and abroad, and in our interactions with our neighbors, so that these terrible choices are no longer needed?

In our own countries, what if we create systems that respond to human need and the painful circumstances that often lead to violence? What if children who are suffering are identified and helped before they turn to violence? What if human needs for food, clothing, safe homes, and loving support are met? What if sharing and caring become more important that amassing wealth or co-opting world resources, without regard for the larger good.

We already have some systems in place. But how are they working? A great deal of money is being spent, but far too many children and adults are falling through the cracks. We have turned over our responsibility to love and serve our neighbors to government agencies. We have abdicated our responsibilities and in the end given away our rights and our freedom, so we didn't have to get personally involved.

One political commentator stated on the internet a while ago when the United States was trying to help Iraq create a new constitution: "Why don't we let them use ours (USA) as a model? It has stood for many years and created a framework for a great country with unparalleled wealth and peace, and besides, we're not using it anymore."

Has anyone noticed that the events of 9/11 created an opportunity for fear to erode the precious, hard-won freedoms of the United States? Does anyone feel safer and happy with the results?

In the New Testament of the Bible, you will find a quote which addresses this issue very succinctly,

Romans: 17-21

> 17 Do not repay anyone evil for evil. Be careful to do what is right in the eyes of everybody.
>
> 18 If it is possible, as far as it depends on you, live at peace with everyone.
>
> 19 Do not take revenge, my friends, but leave room for God's wrath, for it is written: "It is mine to avenge; I will repay," says the Lord.
>
> 20 On the contrary: "If your enemy is hungry, feed him; if he is thirsty, give him something to drink. In doing this, you will heap burning coals on his head.
>
> 21 Do not be overcome by evil, but overcome evil with good."[2]

It is a well-known phenomenon that what we resist, persists. In fact, what we resist grows stronger. Fighting terrorism with terrorist tactics not only doesn't work, but it diminishes us as individuals and as a people.

If you wish to fight terrorism, find that which is in yourself that feeds terrorism and heal it. If you are led to accomplish something in your local or larger community which expands good, do this. Do not give attention, either in yourself or in your outer world, to that which expands any form of negativity.

---

2 *New International Version Bible Online, Copyright © 1973, 1978, 1984 by Biblica.*

The majority of the people of the United States like to think of this as a Christian country. However, far too many are not supporting the principles that I have taught. If there is any question in anyone's mind about what is a Christian action, let me state it very simply. Ask yourself, *"Does it come from love?"* If your choice feeds and expands your heart, then that is Christian. That which feeds and expands the ego is something else.

"Does it come from love?"

As I pointed out in my Palestinian lifetime (more than once) it is not just one people or one religion (Judaism in my time) that exemplifies the Truth.

Anyone who chooses love is acting as I have taught, whether they are an "official" Christian or not. And any Christian who is choosing to act from fear, anger, hatred, revenge and bigotry is not acting as a Christian and is giving Christianity a bad name.

It was once said, "You can tell that they are Christians by their love."

I came not to start a religion, but to demonstrate a principle and to bring forth a new level of understanding of the nature of God – Love – and ultimately of your own nature, which is a unique expression of God. It was deemed best at the time to specify that those people who were acting on these principles belong to a group that was bringing forth a new teaching.

The development of Christianity as a religion and then into many different sects, denominations and variations was a result of too much thinking and not enough love in thought, word and deed.

Indeed, Love is a principle that even the simplest mind can understand and follow. The complications of what and how to believe and act, rules to follow, etc., did not lead everyone to better behavior. And those who should have been leaders were often the least able to demonstrate love.

But despite the errors that have proliferated, I am happy to say that the basic teaching of love is clear in most minds, and those who choose otherwise at least know that they are not serving God or their fellow man/woman/child in the process. No matter how the ego might try to justify it, the Heart knows the Truth.

Bottom line – if you want to fight terrorism, root it out of yourself first, and do it with love and forgiveness. That will enable you to find a path to help the world in a way that is truly helpful and based in Love, not fear.

I wish to speak here of the soldiers who have had to serve in wars and who have been traumatized in soul and body as a result. Please place them in your prayers and ask that they be healed and forgiven in body, mind and spirit.

I suggest this prayer:

For Soldiers Everywhere

Beloved Holy Spirit,
Come to the soldiers of the world.
Heal their minds and their bodies.
Restore their souls to wholeness and peace.

Let light and love fill those places of
    darkness
Which have been the fruits of war.
May they find forgiveness for themselves
And those that they perceived as enemies.

May they grow in compassion and wisdom
Through their experiences.
May they be inspired to act in new ways
That lead to Peace, Joy and Freedom for all.

For World Peace

Beloved Mother-Father God,
Peace is your gift to all on Earth.
May we each honor this gift with
Right living on every level.

Help us to know what is right,
To act in ways that serve the good of all,
To love ourselves and others,
So that Peace may fill each heart and
      mind.

We honor the gifts of the Prince of Peace
By living in such a way that Peace is
      restored,
That love is revealed,
That all are sustained and uplifted.

We give thanks for Peace on Earth.
So be it. Peace. Selah.

I Am Jesus, with you Now and Always.

Chapter 3

The Power and Presence
of the Holy Spirit

Let us begin today with a meditation.

Exercise 1: 3-1 **Clearing with the Holy Spirit**

Go into your hearts, dear one. Allow your heart to expand to new levels of love and understanding. Open yourselves again and yet again until you can see the warp and weft of the weaving of your soul.

Allow the hidden spots of darkness to be released into the Void to be cleansed and returned to the Unmanifest as renewed particles of potential being.

Allow the wind – the Breath of the Holy Spirit – to move through your heart, lifting out the heaviness, opening up that which was constricted, releasing miscreations of darkness, doubt, despair and doom, and removing that which was hidden, and frightening, and repulsive.

As the dungeons of thoughts and feelings are cleansed, allow every cell and atom of your being, on every dimension, in all parallel realities, all time and no time to be filled with new frequencies of peace, love and healing. And know that you are lifted up in consciousness, into the higher realms of love, light and perfection.

Know and feel that this is your new reality. Make a commitment to continue this process of clearing, of healing, of being lifted up into greater and greater light and greater and greater love, peace, joy and prosperity.

14

Make a commitment to sharing the gift that you are – your Divine presents, your Divine Presence – on Earth.

C3✿80

We will speak at this time of the Presence of the Holy Spirit in your lives here on Earth.

For many, this Presence might as well be a ghost, because it seems invisible and unknowable, possibly a figment of the imagination. It was certainly something that seemed intangible and unmeasurable, if not inconceivable. The idea of God as Father could be related to, God as Son as well. Did we not have a living example in Jesus to refer to? God as Mother was not taught in the western tradition of the last few millennia, but Mary, as Mother of God, held that template anyway.

In the last few decades, Divine Incarnations of the Mother have come from India to the West to share their loving presence and expand our understanding of God/Goddess. And in the West have arisen those who also know themselves, and are recognized by others, as incarnations of the Divine Mother Presence and principle.

But Holy Spirit – what is it? How could one relate to it?

Some of the Pentecostals, the "Holy Rollers," the Evangelicals, would find in their ecstatic prayers and hymns and healing services an experience of the Holy Spirit blowing across the congregation as a mighty wind, touching hearts and minds; or others might be "Slain in the Spirit" and knocked over and healed by the power and presence of the Holy Spirit, again as a mighty wind invoked by the anointed healers or preachers.

Some have tried to understand this aspect of the Trinity as the Divine Feminine. Rather, let us re-examine the concept of Trinity as Both Masculine and Feminine.

15

Imagine a Masculine Trinity – Father, Son, Holy Spirit – and a Feminine Trinity – Mother, Daughter, Holy Soul.

One can combine these trinities into the symbol once known as the Seal of Solomon, a six-pointed star of two overlapping triangles, now often known as the Star of David.

Truly there are many symbols of the world religions – the cross, the crescent, the Om, yin/yang, etc. Each of these holds hidden meanings, which we will not go into here. Let us merely say that these symbols truly transcend any one religion. They hold a message that the soul recognizes and responds to in myriad ways that can be explored during meditations over many years and still continue to bear fruit.

But we would return to the concept of Holy Spirit/ Holy Soul as an aspect of God/Goddess/All That Is.

In the book *A Course in Miracles* there are commentaries and daily meditations that begin to remove the mysteries of this Presence, and to make it more understandable, more real to the student.

Let us expand on this Power, this Presence, a bit more. Because all on Earth are being lifted fully and finally into the Fifth Dimension, this Presence will be of more immediate experience to each one. It is worthwhile to develop a living/loving relationship with the Holy Spirit that is based on your own experience, not just something you have read.

Holy Spirit/Holy Soul represents the Power of Grace in action. Many of you have pondered the wonder of miracles – miracles of healing, miracles of changed hearts and minds, miracles of grace in a variety of circumstances. *A Course in Miracles* has at least expanded the idea that miracles are possible in this age, not just in the past of the Bible – the expectation that they are possible for anyone, anywhere, any time.

16

I am asking you to consider the possibility that what we now know as miracles will become an everyday reality. As the Power and the Presence of the Holy Spirit/Holy Soul becomes more real to you as something/someone – an aspect of God – that you can speak with, pray to, relate to, you will begin to develop a relationship that creates seeming miracles in your life.

Even in the Fifth Dimension, this Presence, which is of still higher dimensional realities, is not "visible". However, this Presence is accessible and real, even so. Because the Fifth Dimension represents a level of consciousness as well as a frequency band, we can describe it as a place or field wherein life, thought, and feelings are more clear and more pure. The dross and heaviness of the lower dimensions do not penetrate here.

One of the consequences of this purity is that it is easier to create. As one allows thought and intention to be focused, a surge of energy goes forth into the realm of unlimited potential - *the Void* - and attracts the particles of potential matter, which follow the template of thought and flow into form.

You have been aware, perhaps, that as you transition from the Third to the Fifth Dimension, that your manifesting has become more rapid. It has become more and more important that you pay close attention to what you focus on and how you speak. The concept of affirmations and decrees is becoming well known for creating health and prosperity. The use of intention, attention and guided visualization is known to be a significant factor in healing, sports and life in all its aspects.

In working with the Holy Spirit/Holy Soul as a partner in your creations, you will be adding power to your intentions and your creations.

17

This is why during this time of transition on Earth, there is such a tremendous momentum to clear, cleanse and heal all the thoughts, ideas, and negativities of all sorts that no longer serve you. For these densities that were part of the experience of duality in the third dimension have served to teach the lessons of the importance of clarity and purity.

To expand your creative potential as sons and daughters of God now requires that you live in a field of consciousness that supports your visions and your Divine inspirations being made manifest as whole and perfect. And still, there are higher dimensional realities to achieve even more greatly in the future.

How can you work with the Holy Spirit/Holy Soul now?

Begin as you would with any other Divine Being. If you want to learn to work with Archangel Michael, for example, you call his name three times, and you think of the divine qualities he represents, and you ask for his assistance for protection through prayers and decrees. By regular communication, you begin to know who he is as a personal experience, and what he can accomplish with and for you. That is, you develop a relationship – a friendship – through time, attention, and communication.

It is the same with the Holy Spirit/Holy Soul.

*Here Jesus asked me to include certain prayers that my friend and fellow Messenger, Mary Clarice McChrist, has written which assist in linking energetically with the Holy Spirit. More prayers and links can be found on the website for this book, **www. cordeobooks.wordpress.com,** and on Mary McChrist's website, **www.mother-matrix.com.***

Blessings of the Holy Spirit

O Holy Spirit, Holy Soul,
Thou Art the Dove of Peace,
The Holy Soul, like the Mother,
O Holy Spirit, like the Father.

Thy soft wind blows upon my face.
Some think of you as Spirit – Father,
Some feel you as Soul – Mother.
I feel you as the Comforter,
The Peace Maker – My beloved Friend.

Blow me with your soft wind,
Wrap me in your Divine Mantle,
Clear obstacles before my path.

O Holy Spirit, Holy Soul,
Bring forth your sacred gifts:
Clairvoyance - the all-seeing eye;
Clairaudience - the all-hearing ear;
Clairsentience - the gift of
*   all-sensing, feeling spirit;*
Precognition - knowing before it happens;
Telepathy - mental communication
*   or Heart Streams;*
Healing - gift of the Angels and Archangels;

Stretch us, open us, allow us to feel safe
And to blossom at home, for we do not judge
Or limit our family or neighbors.

Is it deja vu or a dream?
Precognition or as it seems?
O Holy Spirit/Soul open me
Like waves of light on a passive sea.

O Holy Comforter, Being Divine,
Hold my precious Earth design,
That through my life all goodness see,
The breath of God is feeding me.

O come, O come Holy Soul /Spirit blend,
Express through me until the end,
Then withdraw from life set free,
O Holy Ghost you will always be.

With love to the Maha Chohan[3],

I Am

Mary Clarice McChrist

---

3 Maha Chohan (supreme teacher) is the title given to the Ascended Master teacher who is holding the office of the Holy Spirit on Earth.

20

Our Vow of Love

O Father/Mother God, Divine polarity,
Blend with us now,
Your Love and Compassion,
Seal our beings in Your Protection.

Blaze through us Your Light,
Radiance and Power,
That we may attune to Your Oneness.

Bless and keep us,
Within the flames of your heart,
That we be held in perfect union –
Veering neither to the right nor to the left,
    walking the Path directly to You,
O Father-Mother God.

Protect, unfold our Great Love,
Neath the wings of the Holy Spirit,
May we soar with joy,
May we become
The outer symbols and sacred ritual
Of God-Oneness.

Beloved Lord Mary

O Dove of Peace

O Dove of Peace, descend,
Descend upon our hearts.

O Dove of Peace, transcend,
Transcend all less than Thou Art.

O Dove of Peace, blend,
Blend we are now Divine.

O Dove of Peace, send,
Send God's Son and His Design.

Beloved Lord Jesus the Cosmic Christ
© *1992 Mary Clarice McChrist*

For information on Mary McChrist's books, e-books, art
*and audio and video offerings, **visit www.mother-matrix.com.***

☙❧

And we will close for today and we are pleased
that you are pleased with where this is all going.

Blessings to you Mikaelah, all is well.
I Am Jesus, with you Now and Always.

Chapter 4
Clearing Negativity

Up to this point, I, Mikaelah, the transcriber of these messages, was experiencing daily challenges of extreme negativity as I attempted to receive the words. At one point, I basically said, I couldn't go on if things stayed the same. I was concerned that it might affect the integrity of the transmissions. What follows was in direct response to this.

Beloved One,

We are indeed with you now. The We that I refer to is the collective consciousness of Divine Oneness. Be assured that all is well. Allow whatever thoughts and feelings that come up during this communication to be revealed. Anything that you experience as rejection, judgment, condemnation or any other form of negative reaction – allow all to be experienced and expressed. But most importantly allow them to be recognized for what they are – not a real part of you.

This is part of the collective field of consciousness that is now being revealed to you. It was what I, as Jesus, the anointed Christ of God, was confronted with by humanity during my ministry.

This was part of what was required of me to experience, so that I might know and understand what was being experienced by humanity, and what must be overcome in order for my message to be received. Those whose belief systems were challenged by me had to address this within themselves as well.

For some, the love, the teachings and the miracles were sufficient to allow them to rise above this collective field of negativity. Their lives did not offer them so much temptation that they could not move forward.

For others, such as the priests, the Pharisees, and most of the Romans, their sense of self importance was so tied to the status quo, that they did not wish to relinquish their beliefs and the "perks" that their lives offered them in order to experience the Truth and the value of what I was sharing. Their egos were flattered by being "better than" others. Thus the comment about the challenge of a rich man to enter the kingdom of Heaven being more difficult than for a camel to go through the Eye of the Needle (a very low gate into Jerusalem).

So I invite you all to now join with me in clearing these effluvia from yourselves and from the collective field of consciousness for all humanity. These are the energies that directly confront and resist your full planetary Ascension. This may be repeated regularly as more is revealed.

Your accumulation of these energies occurred over many lifetimes, and it is the part of Wisdom that it be released over time, in order for it to be assimilated most clearly by your conscious mind and body.

Exercise 1:4-1: **The Power of the Holy Spirit**

Take a moment and center your attention within your heart. Focus on the breath for a few moments. Allow your awareness to focus on the breath as the Life Force and the Love of God entering and filling you with Peace, Love, and Truth.

Invite and invoke the Power and the Presence of the Holy Spirit, expressing through the Sacred Breath, to move not just in and out of your lungs, but to gently move throughout your entire physical, emotional, mental and etheric bodies, often referred to as the "four lower bodies."[4]

Notice the thoughts and feelings of density and darkness that are revealed to you. Do not judge yourself or anyone else for having experienced these thoughts and feelings. Just notice that they exist and remember that you no longer wish to allow them space in your consciousness.

Now, as you continue to breathe gently and deeply, allow the breath to gently surround each negative thought or feeling completely. Watch as it is lifted up and out of your body/mind field. Perhaps some are connected with hooks or cords to deeper levels or to past memories and are more difficult to release. We then ask the angels to assist in disconnecting completely all that you now desire to remove. And now see them being cleared away freely and completely.

Allow all to move into a cleansing process using the Seventh Ray of Forgiveness, Freedom and the Transmutation of all negativity – **The Violet Flame.**[5] You might wish to imagine a great pillar of Violet Flame into which all negative thoughts and feelings are being transferred for cleansing, prior to being released in full freedom as clear energy, and returned to the levels of pure potential matter in the Void.

If you find that old memories are triggered by this clearing, you might wish to utilize another tool of transformation as well, a Fifth Dimensional **Present Time Wand.**[6]

---

4   For more information go to pp. 59-61 in **Live in Love.**
5   There are many ways to work with the Violet Flame. Explore our website **www.cordeobooks.wordpress.com** or do an internet search for some of the many links to prayers, decrees, invocations, silent meditations, sacred images and more...
6   This tool is introduced by Arian Sarris in her book, **Heart Wisdom - Messages from Aruhatala of Telos**.

Imagine what it might look like to you. Perhaps it looks like a long crystal wand or a stream of light. You may envision yourself holding it and tapping the memories or traumas from this or other lives that have been brought to your attention. This will swiftly and completely release any energies that are stuck in the past and free them (and you) to be more fully in present time.

And now, continuing to breathe in the Light and the Love of God, our Mother/Father, allow yourself to be re-filled with clarity, wisdom and compassion, with peace, joy and healing – indeed, with all God qualities in harmony with you and your personal uniqueness and mission.

In order to complete this process, we ask that it be duplicated for the fields of collective consciousness that surround the Earth. We now invoke the Violet Flame to sweep over the entire Earth, clearing, cleansing and healing the collective negativity in the astral and mental planes. On a soul level, we invite all individuals who wish to share in this clearing to be given full assistance as well. We also ask and command that it be done for all our genetic lineage, and for all times – past, present and future – and for all dimensions and all parallel realities.

And now, I offer you this prayer/invocation to continue to cleanse and raise your consciousness.

The Divine Gift of Ascension

Beloved Mother/Father God,
We give thanks for your heavenly assistance,
As we release all that no longer can remain
Within us or around us,
As we are lifted up

Into the Divine Gift of Ascension
Into the Fifth Dimension.

We freely choose to be aligned with All That Is
– A Real, True and Perfect expression
Of your Grace and Goodness,
Peace, Love and Joy.
Now and Always.
So Be It. So may it be forever.

We will close now and suggest that you spend time in quiet meditation and reflection as you align with this new level of clarity and purity. My Peace I leave with you.

I Am Jesus, with you Now and Always.

Chapter 5

Right Opportunity

Today we will speak of the Peace of Right Opportunity.

'What is that?' you might ask. Allow me to explain this concept to you. It is in fact an aspect of the *Tao*, the great flow of the universal life force. This flow is composed of all life choices, beginning with a thought; then an intention; then actions directed toward the completion; and lastly, the accumulated consequences of the choices.

These are all a series of energies on the inner planes. Some appear to be of minor significance, while others connect millions, if not billions, of people across time and space. Some have speculated on the flapping of the wings of a butterfly touching people around the world. A more obvious example, is the death of Archduke Ferdinand, touching off World War I. Even that example clearly had many threads leading to that more obvious moment.

We wish to elucidate – to make clear to you – the ways in which it is vitally important to control your thoughts as well as your actions as you move into the Fifth Dimension. Long before any actions are taken to achieve a certain goal, your thoughts are moving through time and space and accumulating energy, which can ultimately be directed into form.

The Third Dimension is far more dense, and things accumulate far more slowly and results can take a long time, or be changed in an instant through various significant life choices, or even personal and planetary traumas and dramas.

In the Fifth Dimension things move more rapidly. You don't necessarily have months to change your mind and avert results that you don't want.

Thought energies move through the dimensions of the *Void* (7th, 8th and 9th dimensions)[7], attracting atomic particles with a complementary energy, flow, and spin. They begin to create a unique flow within the larger flow of the *Tao*. When you change your mind, or let go of a train of thoughts and redirect your attention, the earlier flow slowly dissipates and is returned to the random – unless it connects with other similar ideas or flows. In that case, it adds to the momentum that others are generating, rather than returning to the Unmanifest Potential.

In this way, your negative, positive, or neutral thoughts might join with others and begin to take on a life of their own. Thus are born *thoughtforms*, and thus, one has the accumulation of ideas with some substance on the mental planes of consciousness, in particular, those around the Earth.

So what you might have thought of as insubstantial and of no importance, may ultimately contribute to a larger construct which might affect humanity for centuries. Hence, the injunction to stay focused on the positive. From the New Testament we have this recommendation in Philippians 4-8:

Finally, brothers, whatever is true, whatever is noble, whatever is right, whatever is pure, whatever is lovely, whatever is admirable – if anything is excellent or praiseworthy – think about such things.

So, how does this relate to Right Opportunity?

Opportunities are the result of an accumulation of these flows of thoughts, intentions, and actions that are in a resonant synchronicity.

---

7   *See pp. 133-136 in* **Live in Love** *for introductory material on the Void and the expression of the Tao within it.*

Let us say that you think it would be nice to have carrots for dinner. They had to have been planted by yourself or someone else. They had to be watered and cared for during their growth cycle. Factors which include arable land, ownership, weather, labor, harvesting and bringing carrots either to market or directly to the kitchen or even to rot in the field, and so much more, had to come together so that there were carrots to be selected. Every item that contributes to carrots on your dinner table is part of a series of individual flows that all come together in the final product.

As you can see, nothing is really simple. And yet all is based on the same principle of the attractive power of those things which are similar, or compatible, or linked. This attractive, connecting power of the universe is Love.

Peace is the principle of that which flows without hindrance versus that which results in conflict.

Peace is the principle of that which flows without hindrance versus that which results in conflict.

Conflicts of thought, intention, and action create a disruption in the flow. Every child who screams, "I hate carrots!" creates a disruption in the flow of "carrots". Every truck in the distribution network that has engine trouble or a flat tire, creates a disruption in the flow. In fact, it might be a direct consequence of many children yelling "I hate carrots!"

War is the direct result of the convergence of the accumulation of opposing flows. (*For more on this subject see section in* **Live in Love** *on Bosnia, pp. 176-177.*)

Harmony is the combination of flows which join together to create a greater flow, which, while different, are compatible

– essentially all "flowing" the same direction. Examples might include many springs which come together to create a river, which flows ultimately to the sea, or various members of an orchestra who play different instruments, and sometimes different pieces of music, to create a symphonic whole.

So, Right Opportunity is that accumulation of the flows of thoughts, intentions and actions which intersect with your choices to result in the satisfaction of your desire or accomplishment of your goal. Changing your mind disrupts the first flow and starts another.

In the case of getting carrots for dinner, it might include money in the pocket, a vehicle to go to the store, and free time to do so, or it might include a sunny day (you don't want to harvest in the rain), the completion of the carrots' growth cycle and again, time to do the picking. Or in a simpler version, if you've already stored the carrots in the kitchen, you merely have to select the right number, prepare them raw or cooked, and add them to the rest of the meal.

We hope that we are not belaboring this point, although it is extremely important, because it is the principle on which you create your own reality through thought, intention and action.

*This is the principle on which
you create your reality
through thought, intention and action.*

If you have been creating your reality with conflicting thoughts, intentions and actions, needless to say, it is far more difficult to have a successful result. This is the value and power of using Affirmations. Affirmations, prayers and *decrees*, when repeated, create a momentum which adds power to the flow which leads to your desired outcome.

If you desire Peace within yourself and around you, "let your eye be single." Keep your thoughts, intentions and actions in harmony with your chosen principles of living. If your chosen principles of living are in conflict with those around you, there will be no Peace either. Thus one must either refine the principles, corrupt them (a choice that ultimately does not bring Peace because it creates a basic conflict at a soul level), or move to a location or situation where there is a greater harmony of underlying principles.

In the example of choosing a job, look first for those employers or companies who have principles of living that are in harmony with your own. This, of course, implies that you are clear on your own.

Mikaelah describes this, for those of higher consciousness, as looking for Fifth Dimensional work. This can be in any sector of life, but involves working with or for those whose goals, principles, intentions, actions and consciousness are in harmony with your own.

In *The Celestine Prophecy,* it is suggested that one look for the path where there is the greatest light when looking for your highest choice. Other indicators, especially when two people are involved, occur when both individuals are grateful, or whether the choice brings joy or disappointment. Some use a pendulum or body signal to tap their intuitive knowing. Ultimately, we are all on the path of learning to choose well – to learn to choose in each moment that which is better and that which is best. As we learn to listen to our internal cues and external clues, to listen to the whisper of our souls, we improve.

These principles apply equally well to choosing a home, a relationship, or any other activity.

I Am Jesus, with you Now and Always.

Chapter 6

Creating Peace

Blessed Ones, I Am Jesus the Christ of God/Goddess/ All That Is. I come to you today to speak of creating Peace within yourself and within the world.

In reality, Peace already exists within you and within the world. However, you can take an active part in finding the Peace within yourself, opening space for more and in so doing not only directly expanding Peace on Earth, but as well enhancing the momentum of the flow of Peace for your beloved planet.

Exercise 1: 6-1 **Finding Peace Within**

So, let us begin by exploring within yourself. Where does Peace reside, and are there energies also present which are in opposition to the Peace you desire?

Close your eyes and allow your consciousness to explore your entire being. Start at your feet and move throughout the body until you reach your head.

- *Are there one or more places where you notice the energies of Peace?*
- *Is it in a protected place in your heart?*
- *Did you find a bit in every chakra? Was it still or moving?*
- *What was the color?*
- *Were there opposing energies of thought or feeling or even physical discomfort?*

Whatever it is, notice it. Honor your Knowing and bless the presence of Peace within you. Give yourself permission to allow an expansion of Peace. Notice those energies that may be covering it or closing it in. Are they energies of fear, doubt, guilt, sadness, pain, regret?

Bring in the Sacred Breath. In Sanskrit teachings, it is said that we are repeating the name of God with every in-breath and every out-breath. It is taught that the sound of the in-breath, **Hum**, and the sound of the out-breath, **Sa**, can be repeated consciously as the mantra "**Hum Sa**" – translated as "I Am That" – the name of God.

Exercise 1:6-2 Breathing the Sacred Name of God

Make breathing a conscious awareness of the nearness of the Divine in you and with you always. Breathe in. Breathe out. Allow the breath to gently surround and lift the heavier energies and watch them dissolve like a cloud in the sky. Feel any lingering traces moved away by the wind – the breath of God.

We invite and invoke the Presence of God to completely clear any and all negativity returning all energies into the Void – the Unmanifest – for transmutation and recycling.

As you continue to breathe, feel those places of Peace within you expanding now. Notice that as they expand, a greater light grows and glows from the center, adding energy to the expansion, for what you focus on expands.

෴

And the peace of God, which transcends all understanding, will guard your hearts and your minds in Christ Jesus. Philippians 4:7

෴

34

And now move your attention to the Earth. See the energies of Peace within the Earth, upon the Earth and above and around the Earth. Once again, call on the Sacred Breath, and breathe within, upon, around and above the Earth, dissolving all energies of discord, hate and fear, disease and death. Whatever darkness you perceive, allow it to gently diminish and disappear as you merge your Sacred Breath with that of the Great Spirit, or as the Native Americans once called it, Wakan Tanka.

See birds of every sort bringing their beauty, joy and music as they soar across the planet, following the flow of Love and Peace and Divine Grace which touches all life. Notice the trees which hold a great Peace, radiating even greater Peace into their regions as they join in the Great inhale and exhale, the Sacred Breath of all Life. And even the rocks and plains, the mountains and valleys, the oceans and rivers and streams join the dance of Harmony and Peace as the Power and the Presence of God moves from the very core of the Earth through every layer within it, upon it or above it in all dimensions — blessing, lifting, healing. May Peace reign again on Earth.

May Peace reign again on Earth.

You might wish to just sit quietly and experience this feeling, this moment.

You might wish to take some art materials and draw the diagram of what you found – the colors, the feelings, the transformation.

You might wish to put on beautiful music and allow your body to move and dance the change from constriction to expansion, from discomfort to Peace.

Let yourself anchor this knowing of the gift of Peace in body, mind and spirit.

ೞ

*Peace I leave with you, my peace I give unto you:
not as the world giveth, give I unto you. Let not
your heart be troubled, neither let it be afraid.*
John 14:27 *King James Version.*

ೞ

I Am Jesus, with you Now and Always.

Chapter 7

Calling for Peace

Blessed One,

I greet you in the name of Peace

I Am the Elohim of Peace.

I Am Aloha or El o ah.

We wish to specifically engage you in an activity of Peace at this time.

Because the entire planet is working through deep, core issues, and the winds of change are sweeping across the Earth and through the inner planes, and into every life, like a mighty whirlwind, assisting in this process, it is deemed that all might benefit from a greater understanding of the ways of calling Peace into what may seem like tumult and turmoil in your daily experiences.

We invite you to our etheric retreat over Hawaii at this time.

Hawaii has been described to you before, (in *Live in Love*, pp. 187-188) as a place wherein one finds great turbulence as the powers of wind, water, earth and fire come together in constant creative and destructive upwellings: islands emerge and grow, mountains erupt in fiery displays, hurricane winds batter the land and sea, great waves tumble the seas and wash upon the shores. It is also a place of extraordinary and majestic beauty.

From our retreat here, the masters who work with the elemental forces assist in the process of maintaining the atmosphere and structures of the Earth in a way which sustains and supports life. Those beings which are monitoring the Earth share their information and allow us to continuously work to balance enough negativity across the planet, so that life may continue to exist and grow here.

We do as much as is needful, while still leaving mankind with enough, that those with eyes to see and ears to hear might still be learning from their choices and behaviors. Ours is an activity of Divine Grace, without which life could not be sustained on Earth.

We share this with you now, that you might become conscious co-creators with us in this activity.

When there is so much destructive activity, there is the danger of imbalance. Our task is to infuse the energies of Peace in and through these elemental powers, so that all works for the highest good for all.

You have read that Peace is the energy which flows without hindrance versus that which results in conflict.

When the energies of Peace infuse situations of conflict and chaos, the Life, the Love, the Power of God move through, attracting and aligning those energies which can be in resonance. That which has little or no resonance with that which is life empowering is moved to the outer edges of the flow and to ultimate dissolution into elemental particles and waves, and then returned to the unmanifest sectors of the Void. So, that which is life-sustaining increases in power.

Let us take the example of a tornado moving across the land and creating loss and destruction in its wake. Buildings are destroyed; trees are uprooted; some are injured or dead; lives are instantly changed. Many turn to prayer at this time. For some, prayer calls in angels to give specific assistance and protection during such an event.

38

For others, assistance comes in their transition from life in this dimension to the next. For still others, assistance comes as help during a time of rebuilding lives and homes and communities.

One activity that is useful and powerful is prayer for Divine Assistance during such an event. Prayer during and after an event helps each one involved to be given help in clearing that which is within themselves that contributed to the problem. Tornados are often referred to as an "act of God." In that they occur following certain basic principles, one might say that is true. However, it is equally true to say that the accumulated negativity of many individuals can lead to such destruction, really an act of clearing and self-protection, allowing for better choices to emerge.

Of even greater assistance is the use of such activities as the calling of the Sacred Rays to give assistance before such events happen. Clearing emotional and mental negativity in the atmosphere around the Earth allows such events to be averted, either partially or entirely. And this allows individuals who might otherwise be influenced by the collective negativity, to make their choices without the collective influences of others' negative thoughts, ideas and feelings.

Author's commentary:

Well, I had to stop here and clear for about half an hour and then eat some breakfast and read for a bit. Somehow, I didn't expect that a book about Peace, where all I had to do was tune in and transcribe, was going to be so challenging. Little did I know that I was going to have to deal with every negative thing inside myself (not to mention the planetary field.) All that was discordant, dissonant or in any way in conflict with Peace had to be addressed and preferably cleared right away. And not just once, but each day new things needed to be delved into. I imagine it might be the same for you, the reader. Good luck. It reminds me of the saying about old age: "It's not for sissies."

So here is what I did to clear:

First, I took my own advice and breathed. Slowly and completely, I breathed in and out of stuck places, confused, places, uncomfortable and painful places in myself. I noticed that most of my attention was going to the second chakra. I remembered that I had a long, busy day yesterday and been out of town and around a lot of people. Perhaps I had picked up some discord from others.

Perhaps I had, but most of what I was observing in my chakras looked pretty old to me.

*I called on the energies of all the **Rays** to vibrate around and through the chakras to clear, cleanse and heal. I allowed the process to be gentle. I wasn't trying to force anything, but I wasn't backing away from it either.*

*I repeated the **Ascension Rosary prayer.** (See the Glosary for the complete prayer.)*

I did more breathing.

I found my hands moving to different parts of my body to send healing energy through the energy meridians. As someone who has been offering energy healing for over 30 years, I've noticed that my hands seem to know what they are doing before the mind notices and examines it and comes up with a logical explanation of how and why.

I let myself stop when I wanted to and made myself some breakfast.

Really, I enjoy knowing things and being able to share them with you the reader. It is a great privilege to align with Divine Beings and share their messages. It feels as though I am exploring the depths of the Universe.

*Right now, however, I feel like I actually know very little and you probably know quite a few things yourself. This is often the case as we enter new levels of being – that sense that we are rank beginners and that there is an enormous amount to learn. Perhaps you'd like to share some suggestions or ideas from your own inner knowing and connections. Visit **www.cordeobook.wordpress.com** where readers can also share their insights and understandings that contribute to the whole.*

I shall continue later.

Chapter 8

Choosing Peace

The Elohim of Peace continues:

So, now let us return our attention to the great Temple of Peace. It is well to know that we can become distracted or disturbed, and yet we can always return our attention not only to places to which we travel in consciousness, but to those places within ourselves at the center of our being. At this time, we shall do both.

Exercise 1:8-1 **An Etheric Visit to the Temple of Peace**

We allow the I AM within us to give us the assistance to travel to the Temple of Peace. Here we observe the beauty that has been created and held by those dedicated to anchoring Peace on Earth. As we move toward the temple, we observe a large fountain in the front of the building. Bright, sparkling water shoots upward 15 - 20 feet high in large concentric circles almost 50 feet in diameter at the outer edge.

Soon, one notices that there is a underlying play of music that regulates the height which goes up and down in synchrony with the sound. And there are colored lights which are also varying in time with the music.

Sit with this awareness of the pulsing flow for a moment. See it and feel it within your mind's eye. Follow it with the breath or your heart's knowing. Close your eyes here and be with this for as long as is needful.

And now continue.

At one point in the cycle, the music stills, the lights fade, the water is completely still. At this moment, we take a deep breath, inhaling this moment and all that passed before, knowing that Peace encompasses both the movement and the stillness. This understanding and deep attunement with Peace moves through our body, like a wave that allows each part and particle of being to be in greater alignment with all that is Good – all that is God.

And now a guide appears at the large arched doorway and we are invited to enter. Each step is now part of a resonant field. We do not hear the sound of our footsteps echoing; rather, each step is as though walking on a giant organ where there is a deep note played in gentle resonance with a larger chord. We are led to a large empty room at the very center of the Temple. High overhead is a large dome, beautifully but simply crafted. All is very white with an opalescent radiance, very still. At the very center we are guided to a large comfortable cushion. It is as though no matter how many enter here, there is only one of us at the center.

Each sits alone in the center. And each moment of this visit has guided us deeper to the still center within ourselves as well. We sit in silence as long as is needful. A gentle pulse moves from tailbone to the crown of the head and above and out. Waves of light move through us from this central pulse, gently expanding and moving out all that is not in resonance and harmony with our core nature of Peace, Love and Harmony – of Divine Will, Divine Wisdom, and Divine Joy. Waves of color and sound and Divine Presence move through us with this gentle pulsing. Deep Healing of all that has gone before touches every level of our being.

When our time is complete, we rise and gently leave the Temple holding this strengthened core of Peace within us now. And we return our consciousness to our daily lives, fully present and alert. We can return at will.

Chapter 9

Being Peace

Once upon a time a planet was created that emanated Peace. It was a beautiful place. In the creation process, Divine Beings came and blessed it with many and varied gifts. Animals and plants of great beauty and variety were gifts from the stars of this universe.

In many ways its story is like that of Sleeping Beauty, for there was a challenge built into this creation as well. When humanity was birthed, it was destined to be mightily tested. It was challenged to fall into a deep sleep, and a veil of forgetfulness was placed upon the consciousness of all. A great wall of thorns grew around the planet built by the unhappy dreams of those who slept. Many tried to pierce that wall and awaken the people, but none had succeeded.

At a given moment in cosmic time, a unique child was born, whose destiny was to grow and mature outside of that dream and to give the gift of awakening to all those who were ready to let go of the dream and to awaken not only themselves but those around them.

This child was the one who came to be known as the Buddha. Though his consciousness was beyond the dream, still he had to deal with the cumulative dreams that had built up over thousands of years. In piercing the veil of dreams, he allowed a great beam of Cosmic Illumination to enter and be anchored. The light spread and darkness receded.

It was seen, however, that not all could be reached by the Buddha's teachings, and another Cosmic Child was

44

birthed. This one came with an even simpler message – his life was an expression of that message –

Love and serve one another.

See God in each other
and love that Truth, that Presence.

Know that the Kingdom of Heaven is found
within your own core of Being.

Forgive those who seek to harm you for they
are caught in a dream that is not real.

The darkness had grown stronger, yet this child's message added a new dimension. For as each heart was touched with this Love, a new light was kindled within it that could never again be extinguished, and it allowed the soul to forge a path that lead to the fullness of the One Light that burns eternally within.

And still each soul had to choose to turn within to know that light and to allow it to expand and grow. As more and more souls learned to open their hearts and to share this love and light, darkness receded still more.

More children came to be born on Earth to bring their light to cancel the darkness.

And in a time of Cosmic Grace, more and more heard the call to awaken from the dream, to turn within to the light, and to share that with others so that all might awaken.

In coming to know and express the Truth of the Light within that you are, you awaken fully. As you awaken, your Love kindles the hearts of others and more awaken from the dream, and this light of a thousand suns bursts forth in a new day for humanity.

In the light of this new day, darkness disappears, recognized as the illusory dream that it is.

When you choose to awaken, to grow in light, to open and expand your heart, to share your loving Presence, then Peace permeates your life, your essence, and blesses all life.

I bring you Peace, find that Place of Peace and stillness within and allow that Peace to permeate every thought, word, and action.

Peace and Love and Divine Grace
Now restore the Plan on Earth.

Peace and Love and Divine Grace
Now restore the Plan on Earth.

Peace and Love
and Divine Grace
Now restore the Plan on Earth.

PEACE.

I Am Jesus, Prince of Peace

Chapter 10

Anchoring Peace on Earth

Beloved Ones, each day, each moment is an opportunity to choose Peace – for yourself and for one another. These times – at the close of one particularly dark era and the beginning of a tremendously bright one, still require your vigilance and your dedication. Commit yourself each morning to the task before you.

Most of you have developed a morning routine. These tend to include a bath or shower, brushing your teeth, combing your hair, getting dressed and eating a meal. We ask that you add a time of prayer and rededication to this program.

Set your intention to be awake and aware of the challenges that life is presenting to you. Make it your heartfelt prayer that you choose Love, you choose Peace, you choose that which is Life-affirming.

As those aspects of your consciousness that can no longer serve you come forward to be explored and healed and released, choose Forgiveness for yourself and others. As you meet those who are finding these times so difficult, choose to be a blessing, not a stumbling block. Choose Peace. And when you forget, remember as soon as you can, and again choose Peace.

Begin your day with Peace and Prayer.

Sustain your day with Peace and Love in Action.

Complete your day giving thanks.

Complete your day giving thanks for all the blessings that have come to you each moment, through the Divine Grace and dispensation of these times. Know that each one on Earth is being maximally helped to release all that no longer serves.

Sometimes you will be the receiver of this help; at other times, you will be the one who renders assistance to one in need. At all times, remember to call for Divine Assistance to ease the path. For all are facing these challenges, and many have not had your opportunities to learn a variety of tools of transformation to smooth this path and ease the journey.

Earth and all upon her are moving steadily forward. Has there been some painful world event lately? Perhaps you have noticed that they seem to be increasing in number.

Earthquakes, tornados, hurricanes, floods – the media are full of such multiple stories. Send love and blessings and peace to those who are facing life's challenges, large or small. Send Angels to offer support and healing, and to bring their many gifts of comfort to those caught in such events.

Blessed one, know that each one on Earth is being given maximum assistance. As dreadful as any particular experience might seem, know that it has been adjusted to be far less than it might have otherwise been, due to daily activities of Divine Grace. Your prayers at this time are vastly important.

Continue to hold the vision for the highest and the best outcomes for each individual and for all Life within and upon the Earth. Continue to pray for miracles and Divine Grace to ease these times, and bless each person and each situation that comes to your attention. All moves forward magnificently. Know beyond a shadow of a doubt, that you and each one here is being watched over and cared for. Know that the collective consciousness is being cleansed and uplifted. Know that your social systems are being purged, and a new higher order vision is being infused into the hearts and minds of humanity.

Prior to the implementation of these new ways, the old must pass away. That which can no longer be tolerated is being replaced with that which truly serves the whole. New economic systems are emerging. Innovative ways of teaching and supporting the growth of children are becoming the new norm. Politics are being examined minutely. And on and on.

Turn your attention to that which it is in your heart to do. You were divinely designed to carry ideas and visions that are an important part of this transformation process. What is your part? Invite the Angels of Peace, Love, and Healing to help clarify your goals, to increase your courage and commitment, and to sustain your enthusiasm as you direct your energy to the accomplishment of each task along the way.

In these ways, you will be anchoring Peace on Earth – each day, each moment. Intention, focus and commitment. Love and prayer and purpose. Be the Peace.

So be it. I am Lord Jesus/Sunanda[8] – One with you in the Light and the Love of the Christ and the Peace that passeth understanding.

---

8   *After many years of working deeply with Lord Jesus and Lord Sunanda and after many discussions with those who wonder are they the same or are they not, I have come to the conclusion that they are One in the Beingness of the Cosmic Christ. And they each have individual personalities. There is a great deal that I do not know about all this, but I do know that both come from levels of Love and Wisdom that lift the heart and the soul into Union with the Divine and assist in personal and planetary Ascension in these times of Transformation on Earth.*

Chapter 11

One in Peace

Blessed and Beloved One,
Holy Christ in Me,
Blessed One,
Holy Sun,
Beloved are We.

Blessed and Beloved One,
We are One
In Love and Light,
Enraptured in the Sun
And Holy in God's sight.

Blessed and Beloved One,
God in you and me,
Grant us Peace
And Holy Grace.
Love has set us free.

What is Oneness? How can we continue to be the uniqueness of our Individuality if we are merged in Oneness?

These are the questions that the ego, steeped in separation, poses. And yet, they have merit and deserve to be answered.

If the aeons of time devoted to our individuation had a purpose, what is the purpose of this reuniting into One Being again?

It has been revealed in the ancient literature and the memory of it is still available in the collective knowing, that God/Goddess chose to individuate. All individuals know that God is within them – even if this knowing might be removed from conscious awareness.

The Presence that Lives and Moves and Has Its Being in and through us, uniquely expresses through each individuality.

We were created to allow the Divine to fully express through matter / mater / mother – a Divine dance of creation. It is said that there was a war in Heaven over this plan – certain Angels thinking that humans should not have this grace. Perhaps it happened that way. Perhaps that was merely part of the building of the illusion of separation so that individuation could progress.

We wish to refer this to the Divine In-Breath and the Divine Out-Breath. In the great reaches of eternity, God breathes out creation, and breathes it back in again. What this cosmic progress encompasses is beyond the scope of this text; however, the principle it represents is clear enough. The Sacred Breath, the Life and Will of God in expression can be followed. We, as individualized expressions of the Creative Breath, also breathe in and breathe out.

51

Through the flow of the breath we can also harmonize our being, enhance our clarity, realign with Divine Will and merge in the Heart and Mind of the One Presence. We can imagine that we understand the larger picture, but in truth, we are each a piece of the puzzle (a peace of the puzzle?). Our understanding is only fulfilled in the merging with that Oneness.

Through the flow of the breath, we align with the Supreme Consciousness, and in so doing, we enable ourselves to more perfectly express the uniqueness that each were created to be. As we flow in this Consciousness of the One Heart/One Mind, we can more perfectly express our individuality. It is a complex idea, yet a precious and simple one.

As we come to know God within ourselves, we begin to more clearly see God within each other individual. As we honor God/Goddess within, we find delight and exhilaration in observing and participating in this Divine Dance of Oneness.

Breathe in, breathe out. There was once a greeting card with this idea.

On the cover it stated –

"List of 10 things to do today."

Inside – Breathe in, Breathe out.

Breathe in, Breathe out.

Breathe in, Breathe out.

Breathe in, Breathe out.   .

Breathe in, Breathe out.

It seems too simple, but it is the essence of our life. Our existence in form requires this basic activity. Breathe in, Breathe out. Breathe in, Breathe out.

There is a whole Vedic science directed to working with the breath. Athletes are learning its techniques to enhance their performance. Those living too stressful lives are learning to breathe more consciously to calm and center themselves. An old adage suggests we count to ten when angry to find a place of inner calm. Ten breaths taken in conscious awareness of the Divine breathing in and breathing out through us.

Exercise 1: 11-1 **Ten Healing Breaths**

Let us now take ten healing breaths. Ten inhalations of Divine Grace and goodness – ten exhalations of all that no longer serves us. Indeed, do we not inhale oxygen and exhale carbon dioxide with every breath. It is most profound and powerful when we allow ourselves to be conscious of this process. In so doing, we honor the Divine design of our creation and our creativity.

Breathe in Love, release all that is less than love, breath in Peace, release all that is less than perfect peace. Breathe in Joy, release all that is limiting that joy. What a gift! It is ours now. Use it, honor it, bless yourself and all life with each breath.

May we ever grow in Peace and Oneness with all Life.

I Am the Christ, and we are One.

Book Two

LOVE

Chapter 1

Know That We Are One

Beloved Jesus speaks.

Blessed ones who love the Christ, I Am He whom you love. But in this act of loving another, I say unto you, you expand the sense of separation. See rather that we are One. Know that we are One. Know that even the concept of we is separation. Contemplate the Oneness that all is. Allow your heart and mind to expand into and beyond the reaches of time, space and inter-dimensional reality, into and beyond the Void, into and beyond All That Is, into and beyond every thought, idea and concept that you have ever had of Beingness. Here in the vastness will you find your true Self. And know yourself to be the ever-expanding and yet unchanging whole. That is your true nature.

Look not upon sin or error. Place no attention whatsoever on that which is unlike God. Follow the recommendation in the Bible. Stay focused on that which is lovely, that which is good, that which is uplifting for all life. And if you desire to add to that which is lovely, that which is good, that which is uplifting, know that a part of you is already there. A part of you is already lovely, already good, already uplifting and already with every breath expanding the Light and the Love that you are, that All Is.

But, you might say, I wish to help to heal the errors I have created in the past. I wish to serve the planet by clearing the accumulation of error that make up the planetary fields of consciousness. I say unto you, whatsoever you do for the least of your seeming brothers and sisters, you do for all. Do not strive to do great things, but follow the advice of Mother Theresa and strive to do even small things with great love.

For it is love that will correct the errors of the past and heal the hearts and minds of the individualized aspects of the One that we all are. Ask "how can I add love to this world?"

Sit for a moment and be in the stillness.

Let the knowing that all the love there is already *is* here. Mahatma Ghandi said, "Be the change that you wish to see in the world." I suggest that you Be the Love that you wish to see in the world. It is not a matter of adding more love to the world, it is a matter of aligning with the Love in greater and greater measure. In so doing, that Love is anchored on Earth and made more accessible to all.

> *Be the Love*
> *that you wish*
> *to see in the world.*

What must you do to be this Love and allow your consciousness to expand within it in ever greater measure?

Find those places within yourself that you believe are unlovable, unworthy and surrounded with limitation, darkness and despair. Let the Love which is Light and the Light which is Love embrace each and every particle of yourself. Love what you admire; love what you judge as unworthy; ove the mistakes; that which is healthy and that which is damaged; and love the seemingly unlovable.

As you heal the thoughts of unworthiness within yourself, you become a blazing beacon of Hope, a beacon of Truth that touches each person on Earth and indeed throughout the Universe – and beyond that as well. You don't have to fix anything. You don't have to heal anyone. Love alone is enough. There is no prayer, decree or mantra, no act of service or karmic repayment necessary if you just allow the Love that you already are to touch that which is experiencing separation within yourself.

Love is the energy of connection, of bonding, of drawing together. It draws that which experienced a state of individuality – seeming separation – and blesses that which was accomplished in self-knowledge, self-awareness in this state. Love calls you to return to oneness and to remembrance of the wholeness and perfection that you are.

Miracles result from that restoration to your Divinely created perfection – basically a removal of your attention from a focus on wrongness and error to that which is whole and perfect. When I, Jesus, healed in what seemed miraculous ways, I saw what was the highest vision of wholeness for an individual and allowed their energy bodies to be reunited with that wholeness. I focused only on the wholeness, saw only health and the original expression of God through each one, which allowed the physical body to be realigned into health.

If you wish to help the planet, love yourself, and love your neighbor, who is another facet of the Divine Oneness that is also yourself. It is love that is the final test and healing and resolution into wholeness for the Earth in this time of transition.

Do you see things that make you feel it will take a miracle to correct? Allow yourself to know that miracles are completely natural. They are a result of clearly holding Love and Truth more strongly in your Heart/Mind than whatever error you seem to see around you, which is an illusion brought about by delusion. Keep your attention on the good.

We shall end this section with this Biblical quote from Paul.

ᘓᘔ

"Finally, brothers, whatever is true, whatever is noble, whatever is right, whatever is pure, whatever is lovely, whatever is admirable - if anything is excellent or praiseworthy - think about such things." Philippians 4:8 NIV

ᘓᘔ

Chapter 2

Oneness

Beloved One,

Let us speak today of Oneness. For it is only in our Oneness that we are truly whole. Anything less than that Oneness, leaves you with a sense of incompleteness. You know the souls who seem to never have enough, get enough. You label them vampires, energy suckers. You see the results around you in the world of those who seek to pull resources to themselves. The seemingly unending need for more oil, more gold, more money, more power, more attention, more love. These ones are seeking in all the wrong places to fill the void within themselves.

How can that emptiness be filled?

There is no need. That which appears empty is already full. What is needed is a change in perspective. If you look at the sky in the daytime, it appears empty. At night you can easily see that it is filled beyond measure with stars and beyond your vision with even more planets and lifeforms than can be imagined.

So it is with every place of seeming emptiness.

Perhaps you look in your wallet and it appears empty. Know that that is only one perspective. As you focus on lack, you multiply it. Focus rather on all the money that may have already passed through it, knowing that it is a continuous ebb and flow, not a final thing. Allow yourself to imagine the money that might come to you from known or unknown sources to fill it even in the next minute.

Even the wealthiest might spend all that is in a wallet or purse, but they know that there is more where that came from or that they can easily replace it or recreate it from scratch if necessary.

Allow yourself to receive all the good that is coming to you every day, every moment. Sometimes that good is in a smile, sometimes in a happy thought, sometimes a rhyme you chant as you pick up a penny. "See a penny. Pick it up. All the day, you'll have good luck." How might that create a different mood, a different path than, "Oh, a penny, that's not worth the trouble to pick it up."

A famous comment from Henry Ford when asked what he would do if he lost all his millions, he responded, "If I lose everything in the collapse of our financial structure, I will start in at the beginning and build it up again."

What stories are you telling yourself every day?

Perhaps you look at your heart and it feels empty, torn, broken, unloved and unlovable. An empty shell – a burned-out field. But the truth is that every cell and atom of your being is created and held in love. Every breath you take comes from love.

So, start with the breath. Breathe in the Life that sustains each and every being on Earth. This planet is sustaining billions of life forms. Honor life in each plant and fish and bird. Each rock and mineral has its journey of being and becoming. We live surrounded by miracles. Each seed that grows and becomes a flower or produces fruit. Each birth. The infinite variety and richness of life expressing. Each seeming death that leads to experiences on other planes of reality. You are a precious part of that infinite life expressing. And with every breath, you share that life with all on Earth.

It is in judging the experiences of a particular moment that you forget the glory that surrounds you. Perhaps you are presently living in an extremely difficult set of circumstances, surrounded by death, destruction, disease or depression. Merely by taking a moment to focus on your breath, on the love that fills and sustains you every moment, you can allow that love to be shared. For love shared is love multiplied. In sending thoughts and feelings of love into seeming darkness, you can be a force for change.

Mikaelah once lived in Berkeley and there was a man who was going around burning buildings. The papers were full of stories on the places burned – a field, a house, a church. Who was doing it? Why? Mikaelah began to dream that he was coming to burn down her house. After the dream repeated several times, she knew that continuing to focus on this with fear could actually bring it to her. So she went to a friend and asked for help.

She had just begun studying metaphysical ideas at this time, so she had a few tools to work with.

The friend suggested that she ground herself, make a heart connection and send unconditional love to this man.

Mikaelah was terrified at the thought of connecting with him. But she felt she must proceed, so rather than a simple energy grounding cord from the base of her spine into the Earth, she visualized calling in golden light from heaven and creating miniature grounding cords from every cell in her body. Each cord was sent deep into the very center of the Earth. Then she felt safe enough to continue. Next she visualized a heart connection from her heart to the heart of this man, whoever and wherever he was.

What she saw next astounded her. The heart she saw looked to her like a burned-out field. She felt so much compassion at the devastation that this man must feel, that she was easily able to imagine sending a stream of love to this poor, devastated heart. As she sent loving energy to this man, she suddenly saw a single flower grow and bloom in that burned-out field. She was deeply touched and felt complete for the moment.

She continued to send love to this man every day. All stories in the paper about arson stopped. No more fires were set. After about six months, she stopped and her mind turned to other things. The fires began again, reported in the papers. She again prayed and sent love. The reports of fires stopped again. Perhaps it was only a coincidence. Perhaps love does make a difference. Perhaps you could send love to situations that concern you. Perhaps you will also see coincidences. Of one thing we can assure you, sending worry doesn't work.

Episcopalian Bishop James Pike of San Francisco once offered this tongue-in-cheek comment on prayer: "When I pray, coincidences happen. When I don't, they don't."

We wish to add one final thought here. When you spend time sending love to various situations that seem to call for it, you may find that you need to access a bigger supply. That need will call forth a solution. You will find that the universe responds by leading you into the next level of consciousness, where you have access to greater levels of love and greater wisdom.

So, do not be concerned that what you have to give is too little or too late. Your love, given freely, is God's grace uniquely qualified as only you can do. In sending that gift out you are completing a great cycle of love. From God to you, through you to another, back to God. In this cycle you are once more a conscious part of the One.

Chapter 3

What is Love?

What is Love? Many of you have experienced the feeling of loving a parent, a friend, a child a special someone. Is that the completeness of love? Have you ever said I love chocolate, I love your hair, I love those shoes, I love that sunset, I love God?

What is the meaning here? Is any or all of this really love? If I say love is the quality of God that is the "magnet" that draws things together, the "glue" that holds them together, then does this explain what love is any more than the above examples?

Let us add to what we have said, by saying that love is the recognition of God in another person, thing or experience. In seeing that combination of qualities that help you remember the nature and the presence of God, you feel the Love in you that resonates with the Love that God is. Seeing God in another creates a feeling of wanting to be even closer, and to have this experience for longer periods and more frequently.

Mother Theresa's idea of seeing Christ in each person was a way of deeply connecting with the Love and other Divine qualities that God is expressing in each one and feeling and knowing that Presence more clearly.

What is the purpose of knowing what Love is, and how can feeling Love as a quality, an energy, a particular Ray of God help us as human beings? To feel love is an almost universally desired experience. To feel love filling your heart and mind creates a great feeling of well-being. Indeed, even at the cellular and atomic levels, love is experienced and creates greater functionality.

By this we mean that love actually helps you not just to feel better, but to be better. At the atomic, cellular, organ, system and whole being level there is a realignment with the better and best form and function, ultimately with being and expressing the highest "you" that can be.

Ultimately, it is love that allows you to so remember God that all separation ceases, and you become again that which you love. On Earth, this means that God is expressing uniquely through you as God in form.

This does not mean that you can start judging anyone not in seemingly perfect form, as not being loving enough. Each person comes into form in order to achieve a number of goals: learn lessons, clear personal, planetary and universal karma, grow in certain areas, and serve through their gifts and talents. There are opportunities to choose, to make mistakes, to choose differently, to succeed and to fail. Some of those who experience disease and suffering are taking on pain for others. There are many lessons here as well.

Let us engage in a little exercise here, because this is an all-too-common problem for many. They unconsciously identify or sympathize with another's pain and take it on. Because this is done unconsciously, they often do not have the tools to actually clear the pain and suffering. They have just moved it around.

Let us offer an exercise that will allow you to identify what you might have picked up from another and to release it in such a way that no one else is harmed.

(This exercise can be done anywhere, anytime, but to begin, it might be best to be sitting and to have some uninterrupted time. It can be done individually or as a group.)

***Exercise 2:3-1* Clearing Another's Emotional Energy.**

First, just sit quietly and breathe gently and peacefully. Grounding yourself is helpful. You might imagine a cord of light, which extends from the base of your spine going into the center of the Earth and attaching firmly. This helps to center you and to bring you into the present moment.

Call on your Higher Self and Angels of Healing to come and be with you. Next, let your awareness move around your body. Notice any pain. Where is it located?

*It is often helpful to imagine a large, clear crystal bowl in front of you. First ask that any pain or energies that are not your own be moved out of your **four lower bodies** (physical, emotional, mental and etheric) into the bowl.*

Focus first at your feet, and move your attention slowly upward, watching as energies are gently moved away from you and into the bowl. If some energies or dark areas seem to linger, ask the angels to assist in their removal.

Now, observe the energies in the bowl. Are they cold, hot, dark, prickly, sticky, murky?

*Just notice what they look or feel like, and remind yourself that you had that in you. No wonder you didn't feel terrific. Next, call on the 7th Ray energy of **Violet Fire** to completely purge and transmute all the energies in the bowl. Allow them to go where they need to go now. If there is still pain and/or darkened areas within you, ask the angels to assist you in letting go of your own pain and trauma, any dark energies from any lifetime. Let that go into the bowl, and again call on the Violet Flame to transmute all karma and negativity that lead to pain and suffering for you or others.*

Again ask the Angels of the Violet Flame to assist.

Now allow yourself to stand in a rainbow of colors – each representing different Divine Graces. These will fill you with light that is in exact harmony with you and what is most beneficial for your health and well-being. All energies that have moved out are now replaced with clear, healthy light.

Let yourself sit now, bathed in light, opening like a flower to the sun. Drink in this gift from God. When you are full to overflowing, then it is appropriate to share this bounty with others. Send gifts of love and light to those who are in need. Perhaps there are those you know who need this gift. Perhaps there are those that the angels know need this gift. Fill yourself with light; share it with others; and set your intention that there is a never-ending flow filling you constantly, restoring you to health, and restoring you to the knowledge of your oneness as you share your blessings with others.

Send prayers and light to those who are ill, to those who are troubled, to those who need clarity, to those who have recently crossed over, to the loved ones left behind. Send light and love to those whose world is entirely different from yours, and to those who might live next door or down the street.

Is there a right way to send light or love? The right way is the way that blesses you as it blesses others. The right way is the way your heart is inspired to share, the way your imagination leads you.

೮೫೮೦

And let us close this chapter with a prayer.

Send Your Light

Dear Heavenly parents, angels, guides and
    teachers of the Light,
There are many people who are suffering,
    many who are lost.

Please send your light, your healing, your
    peace and your love to all who are hurting.
Bring the gifts of illumination to those who
    can benefit best from that.
Bring light of wisdom to those whose needs are great.

Bring your great love to heal the wounds of body,
    mind and spirit.
Bring miracles to those who have lost faith and hope.

Bring forgiveness to those who cannot
    forgive themselves.
Bring joy when all life seems dreary.
Bring your gifts to each and every soul,
In perfect measure for each need.

We thank you for every angel, every friend,
Every tree and flower, every breath,
Every gift we receive each moment of each day.
We thank you for life, and love and miracles.

May we all rejoice in the wonders of creation.
May we release all that no longer serves us and
Open to new levels of God's grace at exactly
    the right and perfect time,
And in the right and perfect way.

Thank you for those who have helped us on
our journey.
And thank you for those we have been
privileged to help.
Thank you for all the good.
Just, thank you.

க்ஜூ

Author's note. Jesus asked me to share this personal reflection on enlightenment here:

Esoteric literature speaks of our need to qualify all the energies or rays with our emotional energy as we use it. Our free will chooses to create joy or pain in what we share with others.

The most powerful exercise I learned was to imagine my heart filled with the Universal light of Love and send a beam from my heart toward anyone I wished.

The results were beautiful, but never the same. Different people saw different colors and images every time. I saw that I could draw from this Infinite source and need never be diminished. In the beginning stages, I found it difficult to both send and receive. So, sometimes, I did become depleted. But always I was reminded to return to the Source and to drink freely and deeply of all that I could hold. An amazing lesson plan began to unfold before me. As I began to realize there was tremendous joy from sharing this Love, I chose to give more and more freely. The more I was able to give, the greater became my ability to both hold this Love and to share it.

This was the first step for me in the Awakening process. With each new expansion of my ability to Love, determined by my choices, and actions, as well as God's plan for me, I found that there was a simultaneous expansion of Consciousness. These expansions were experienced as Initi-

ations which were most often visualized as stepping through a doorway into so much greater light that I was often unable to see at this level for several weeks until my body had adapted somewhat.

With each expansion, I could also physically feel the light vibrations of my body being lifted. It felt as though the very cells and atoms were on fire. This sensation lasted a few weeks until my body adjusted. This, I was told was the path of Enlightenment.

Some people have expressed the opinion that Enlightenment is not a series of gradual steps but rather a process that happens all at once. I would answer that both experiences are true. In the first case, the individual experiences a growing expansion from one step or initiation to the next in a process of spiritual evolution.

In the second, the individual has been born having already earned some level of expansion (attainment) in previous lifetimes. At the right time for their particular lifestream, they are awakened to the full awareness of it.

I have written more on this subject in my book **Live in Love – A Life Handbook for the New Golden Age**, where I cover levels of Initiation and information about both human and angelic cycles of Ascension that is not available elsewhere, but which is based on my personal experiences as led by Jesus and other Ascended Masters.

Chapter 4

Capturing the Essence of God

Beloved One, we are with you now and always.

Do you feel alone and abandoned? Do you feel as though nothing you write is good enough? Do you feel that you haven't really captured the essence and flavor of the Light and the Love that God wishes to reveal in this book?

What is it that you feel is missing? It is that grace and glory that speaks the Name, the Essence, the Treasure and the Pleasure that God/Goddess is to you. That is what you hope and desire to share. That sense of the ineffable, the numinous, the Great I Am That I Am which lives and moves and has its Being within each of us and in all Life.

Are there any words that can convey the depth and the height and the breadth of that Love? Can we even begin to understand what Love created this Earth, the multitude of stars in our galaxy and solar system, the infinite array of atoms and molecules, the splendor and miracle that is even a single human being, a flower or an ant?

Words can only hint at the glory that the heart and mind strive to examine and to experience. And yet, even as you write, or perhaps as you read, you can feel the warmth and the light and the unique flavor of love that fills your heart and your soul.

For each one experiences love in ways that only their combination of DNA, molecules, cells and organs, body and soul, color of skin and hair, length of legs and arms, fingers and hands, flexibility and strength, memories and experiences can know and understand.

And this variety is multiplied a million, billion times on every planet, star, galaxy and universe. And still the heart and the mind insist, it can be known, I can experience this, understand it, express it, for I AM THAT!

And so, we each strive to know and understand that Love of which we are a unique expression. We seek that love outside of ourselves. We see beauty, and we seek to own it, to possess it. We see goodness, and we admire it and perhaps seek to copy it. We see the benefits of wealth and power, and we can be caught up in having more and more. And always it seems to be outside of us.

Turn to yourself for a moment. See the beauty, the goodness, the wealth and the power that you infinitely are.

Do not focus on that which is not. See that which is. Even a single cell is a miracle and a wonder. Know your own beauty, your goodness, your Divine inheritance of strength and wealth and power, truth and love, wisdom, and honor and so much more. In this understanding and exploring, you know God more deeply and can begin, only begin, to comprehend the magnificence that Love is.

If you feel that this book, these words cannot possibly encompass the moon, know, at least, that it is a finger pointing toward it.

So, we simply say, know that you are Love in form. To know God, look within. You are the microcosm of the macrocosm. You are the hologram. Each piece is a perfect expression of the whole. If you seek to love God, Love yourself. Love your neighbor.

If you seek to love God,

Love yourself.

Love your neighbor.

71

As you extend love, you come to know the Nature of God more thoroughly, more deeply. An old song once expressed this idea: "To know, know, know him, is to love, love, love him."

Chapter 5

Christ Consciousness

We will be speaking of Christ Consciousness now.

This is a complex subject, and yet it is that which demands your attention at this time, because that level of consciousness to which the planet is ascending – the movement into the Fifth Dimension is exactly that. It is a movement into Christ Consciousness.

It is said that in my lifetime as Jesus at the time of Roman rule in Palestine, I came to be a living template of that future which this planet is now entering.

So, what is your concept of that lifetime? Do you see it as something to be admired or desired? Do you see it as something that is beyond anyone's possible achievement? Does it sound as though some of those things couldn't possibly have happened and must have been made up? Does it seem as though, yes, you can believe that those things were real, but so difficult of attainment that you might as well not hope to achieve anything like it yourself? Does it seem that religion has served to create more confusion rather than a true assistance to live a better life?

If you are reading this book, you may feel that you believe that all things are possible, and that you yourself might just be able to achieve the miraculous, and yet, are there not places within yourself where you prefer not look? Are there not places that seem so dark or distorted, that you'd rather ignore what hides there than to even admit that such exists?

73

We ask you to love yourself enough, even the parts that hold terrible pain and suffering, so that together we can look at these areas of density and allow the light of awareness and attention to be directed there. Only by being willing to see what needs to be corrected, can one be fully prepared to move forward now.

The period you have been passing through since the opening of the stargate during the Harmonic Convergence on August 17-18, 1987, has been a time of extremely rapid acceleration of planetary frequencies. Each individual has been experiencing change, transformation and accelerated learning and healing. That which no longer serves is being brought into full awareness to be healed and released. Each one is examining his or her own life.

Not all are able to be completely honest with themselves. There are some who have taken on the task of expressing outwardly what others are denying within themselves. It doesn't always look too pretty. There is a lot of judgment flying around about others. It is time to stop running away from the dark.

We do not suggest that you wallow in the darkness, but you must acknowledge that it exists in order to be willing to bring the light of awareness to it. You must be willing to allow love to clear away the wounding and the distortion, so that the Truth of what is Real can restore all of you – all that you are – to your own identity of perfect man, woman and child.

Because you are all mirrors for one another, you need only look to your group of friends, family and acquaintances, to begin this process of healing that which has been hiding in plain sight.

Have you had a strong desire to tell a friend or acquaintance or family member what you would like to see corrected? Are they cruel, rude, tacky, obsessed with "things," careless of the feelings of others, etc? This, then, is *your* area of growth.

We ask that you start with one person at a time. Think of all that you see needs to be corrected. Accept that this is a mirror for you. Allow angels to bring waves of love to the person you started with and to yourself in any way that this area needing correction is maintained in or around yourself, your energy field, your memories or etheric records.

Let love gently and perfectly reveal and heal any error that you have seen.

If you have a friend who you consistently admire, enjoy, appreciate and feel good around, give thanks that this is also who you are. If you feel that way about all of your friends, families and acquaintances, look a little farther afield. Anyone whose behavior causes you to be upset or judgmental, for example a politician, professional person, public servant, head of a large corporation, member of the military, public figure, etc. can be an opportunity for noticing what needs to be healed.

For indeed, we are each a microcosm of the macrocosm. Bringing love to that which is in error is necessary now to clear the accumulated error in the planetary field. This is not about dwelling on what is wrong; it is about loving ourselves back into our full perfection.

And when you begin to look at each person as someone who is worthy of love, remember that you are also worthy of being loved, indeed, that you are love. And because love is your nature, it is natural to extend it to others. In so doing, you become an even more integral part of the transformation process of Love revealing itself to itself, of planetary ascension into Christ Consciousness and Oneness.

You Are Love

Revealing Itself to Itself.

Chapter 6

Christ Consciousness Continued

Beloved One, let us sit for a moment in the Oneness, in the Allness, and from the place of wholeness, notice that you are also a being of unique expression and understanding. From your individual expression you are refining your ability to align with Highest Purpose, so that every thought, word and action, might serve to uplift and enrich the whole.

The more perfect your alignment, the deeper and more intense is your experience of the Divine energies – Grace, Love, Wisdom, Peace, Joy, etc. – transiting through your nervous system, filling and enlightening every cell and atom, raising each particle of being within and around you into greater heights of perfection.

Thus, Christ Consciousness is a state of ever-expanding perfection and Oneness.

It is said that I, Jesus, was immaculately conceived, as was my mother, Mary. By this it is meant that I came into the world without the distortion of error and accumulated negative karma that most experience. Rather, I came to Earth with certain divinely ordained gifts that were to be of assistance in achieving my mission.

As well, my mother, Mary, held a field of conscious perfection around our household. Thus, I was little contaminated by the negative thoughts and feelings that humanity exuded, which was filling the energy field around the planet during my childhood.

As I grew, I was required to learn to hold this field of perfection around myself and my companions wherever I was. Thus, when I began my mission, I had thirty years of learning to hold this field, no matter what the circumstances.

I tell you this because it is this that you each are desiring to accomplish as you yourselves move into Christ Conscious communion with all. This is the reason that you are reminded to guard against gossip, criticism, complaining – indeed, any focus on negativity. It is for this reason that the gift of the *Violet Flame* to transmute all negativity has been released unto you, to use and to share with as many as you might. It is for this reason that you have incarnated on Earth.

That which you have chosen to clear within yourself is that which you are clearing for the planet. It is not that you are so damaged or so terrible. It is that you are so courageous as to take on this error in order to correct it for the whole.

Dear Ones, if you see and notice these places of error needing correction in one another, allow yourself to bless this one for their act of faith and courage in taking on such a challenge. Call on Angels to come to their assistance in addressing it, as was their original intention. Pray, not that they be "fixed," but rather that they remember their mission, and be able to receive the love and divine assistance needed to correct and heal the error. Pray that all resources they need might be available to them, and that they might see and be able to receive this help.

If you wish to pray for the many who are daily facing these challenges, ask that angels come to bring them every needed assistance. Pray that they be filled with renewed courage, faith and hope each day. Pray that they might be renewed in their own sense of perfect alignment with Divine Right Action in all their tasks and accomplishments. Pray that they might appreciate themselves and feel appreciated for all that they have taken on. Pray that they might be blessed so as to know and love themselves and one another.

And we say to each of you who have taken on this mighty task, you have succeeded beyond what was believed possible. Earth has reversed its downward trajectory, and your assistance was important. Now the momentum is allowing Earth and all humanity to move forward on their own Ascension path.

Each life stream is daily moving into great conscious awareness of themselves as worthy of all goodness. While there is much focus in the media on that which is wrong, we suggest that you notice the underlying message, that such wrongness can no longer be ignored. We no longer turn a blind eye to cruelty and pain inflicted on others.

Some are drawn to address such problems. They cannot just sit and watch or hear about them without being moved to action that will inspire, uplift and heal. In short, the energies of Christ Consciousness that now are expanding for every man, woman and child – indeed for all life – are infusing the hearts, and minds and will of each one to higher and higher choices, to better and better visions of what might be and how they might participate in achieving that reality.

Let Your Prayers Call
The Problem Solvers into Action

When the media focus on the problems, let your prayers call into action those who are to be the problem solvers. We are all part of the problem, and we are all part of the solution. Pray daily that each need is met with perfect assistance.

Each prayer that comes from your true intention for health, wholeness and Divine Right Action is important.

78

There is no need for one perfect prayer that you should use rather than the simple truth and hope within your own sacred heart. There is no need to look outside yourself for an answer. Allow the Divine Essence within you to lead and guide you forward, to fill you with the perfect words and the perfect vision of what might, and definitely can, be achieved.

Yes, it is both needed and helpful to join with others in chanting sacred decrees, mantras or songs, or in group prayers for sacred purpose. However, we suggest that you learn to trust and know what is right for you in every given moment.

Learn to trust and know

what is right for you in every given moment.

Group work adds immeasurably to the transformation process. There is a time to work together consciously. And there is always the possibility of linking into the group field of conscious service, even when you are seemingly by yourself. But first and foremost, must be your own awareness of what is right timing and right action for you. For it is only from this true sense for yourself that you can truly offer your highest and best assistance within a group.

It is time to so know, love and trust the Divine essence within you, that your belief in your own guidance leads you forward most safely, most efficiently, most clearly.

From this place, your next step is in group formation with those of like consciousness. As you all grow in conscious awareness of and oneness with the larger group Oversoul, you learn the nature and purpose of true group work. As you learn to work together in Conscious Oneness, you each hold a template of oneness that affects everyone around you which helps to build the entire planetary field of oneness.

There are such groups now forming all over the Earth. There are reasons why religions have formed, as there was a striving for this unity of vision, hope and purpose.

The errors held by individuals that created stress and division within any given group, were soul lessons for all, in what must be cleared in order for true unity to develop. Businesses, corporations, religions, governments, nations, guilds, co-ops, boy and girl scout troops, and certainly families were all lessons in the great coming together that is today reaching a time of climax.

Earth's mission, if you will, was to host individuals at the maximum level of diversity of levels of consciousness, indeed, even of physical form (such as animals, plants, and minerals, as well as various angelic, human and elemental races, and the more obvious, skin color, height, and other physical variety. Each was to learn to transcend the physical, emotional, mental and spiritual differences and to know, love, and honor the essential Oneness – indeed, to learn to move beyond even that, to fully and cooperatively allow that Oneness to lead us, in ways we now can barely imagine, into new levels of growth, health, and creativity.

Our orchestra has been tuning up for millennia. The time approaches for the living performance of a magnificent work that will inspire and uplift entire galaxies and universes. For many stars, galaxies and universes have contributed to this living laboratory that we call Earth. And all are watching and learning and growing from the lessons that those on Earth have explored and accomplished.

We have not yet fully emerged into the Fifth Dimension. And even then, there will be that which is still potential. For we, as individuals and as collective parts of the whole, are infinitely exploring the good that is possible in ever greater measure.

Let us close here with a blessing for all those whose lives and sacrifices and lessons have led us to this point and for all universes that have contributed to this living laboratory that we call Earth. And all are watching and learning and growing from the lessons that those on Earth have explored and accomplished.

We bless all who will move forward into the next phase of our evolving greatness and for all who will choose different paths. May each grow in love, in wisdom, in ever expanding perfection for the greater whole.

We are complete for today.

Chapter 7

Circles of Conscious Oneness

Blessed Ones, We are each and all one in the Oneness that is the Allness. Like concentric circles, we stand within circles of consciousness. The first circle is that which defines each one as unique, whole and complete within itself. The next is the circle that defines your closest relationships with friends and family, then the circle of the community within which you live your life. Then there are the larger circles that define country, race, creed, species and planet. The circles extend to solar system, galaxy, and universe. And still further circles extend up to All That Is, and still beyond that as well.

And equally, you stand within concentric circles of consciousness; and as your Love and Wisdom and Will extend into and through and beyond each level again, your heart's wisdom and mind's knowing extend into and beyond All that Is. There you find an interconnectedness with all others at these levels. It is in the awareness of consciousness at these ever greater levels that you come to know Oneness with all life.

And what is the purpose of this growth in consciousness? We chose separation/individuation to know ourselves more deeply. We now choose Oneness, to love ourselves more completely.

We chose error so that we might build strength and character to find the ways individually and collectively to correct it.

We chose separation/individuation
to know ourselves more deeply.
We now choose Oneness,
to love ourselves more completely.

We chose pain and suffering, so that we might be inspired to make better, healthier choices, and sometimes, so that we might more deeply understand the underlying reasons that caused others to choose in these ways. All lessons have been those of learning to understand, to know, to love more deeply, and to find the means of healing and correcting that which had become damaged in the learning process.

And thus, we come to the next book in this series, "Healing."

BOOK THREE

HEALING

Chapter 1

What is Health?

Blessed one, let us begin this third book and this chapter with a discussion on what is health, because, in order to accomplish true healing, one must understand what the nature of true health is.

True health is the perfect outpicturing of the Divine Blueprint for any individual in any kingdom of Being. The Divine Blueprint is the template of your perfection. It resides in the fifth layer of the auric field, the Christ level. Here are the patterns laid down for both the physical body type – height, weight, eye color, race, optimal organ function and so on.

Each person comes with certain karmic responsibilities to complete, as well. These are held in the fouth layer of the aura, sometimes called the etheric, to permit certain physical or mental challenges to be dealt with in a given lifetime. As well, the personality characteristics and the mental gifts and abilities which will most enhance your personal life goals and mission are also on this level which is a vibrational frequency as well as a level of consciousness.

How you use your gifts, the choices of diet, exercise, work, relationships and so on, as well as the experiences of your life which help to create certain fixed belief systems as well as habits of thought, speech and action, all may enhance or diminish your physical, emotional and mental health. In addition you are subject to various life situations and environmental factors, which will further impact your health.

So you, as a human alive on Earth, are a created being influenced by both nature and nurture. You presently have a certain level of healthy function, and have most likely acquired a certain amount of damage and dis-ease over the course of your lifetime.

Where does one begin in the process of attaining greater health and well-being, and realigning with the blueprint of your perfection?

It is most effective to begin with that which is most obvious. If it is in your face, it is the optimal time to deal with it. If you have a cut, clean it and stitch or bandage it. If something is broken, realign the pieces and hold it together until it is mended. Please notice here that the body itself repairs the cut or the broken bones. Your job is to ensure that the parts are held together so that natural state of healing can progress. So, we expect that you are not so much worried about the obvious things that you know how to deal with, but with the deeper issues which underlie the restoring to health.

Exercise 3:1-1 Aligning with the *Divine Blueprint*

Perhaps the simplest and yet most thorough method is to allow your consciousness to begin to once again consciously align with the in-breath and out-breath of the human body and soul. In so doing you still the mind, deepen your connection with Source and align with the breath of the Holy Spirit. So, spend a few minutes focusing on the breath.

Allow your consciousness to become more and more deeply aware of the physical body. Imagine the flow of the breath moving throughout head and body, arms and legs, hands and feet. Notice the flow of blood and breath throughout all of the body. Know that there are nerves and muscles, bones and organs, cells and atoms. All are going about their tasks at even the most minute level.

*Now, imagine and intend that a connection of white light flows from each cell and atom of the physical form, through the levels of the aura. Through the physical, the emotional, the mental, the etheric into the fifth layer, which we will call the Christ level. By sending these links through all the vibrational frequencies that make up the four lower bodies into the fifth level, you allow all four lower bodies to link into the **Divine Blueprint** of your perfection. This allows your body to remember its original Divine Design and to gently correct error and restore itself to perfection.*

*When you have read further, you may link this exercise with use of the **Miracle Wand** (Chapter 5) and freely explore what can be accomplished.*

 C380

Next, Jesus speaks to me, the messenger/scribe, but reminds the reader, as well, of the larger issues we are all facing. If my issues are not yours, substitute that which feels appropriate for you. In many of the chapters, he begins with some issue that I am dealing with and then quickly expands it to that which applies on a much larger scale for humanity. He then lifts the whole field of focus from the lower octaves of consciousness into the sacred.

This project is in fact a form a healing for you in a variety of areas. We would like to point out to you that you yourself have been engaging in a good deal of negative self talk, hiding by retreating to books and computer games, choosing to eat reflexively rather than consciously, and cutting back on needed exercise. These have been balanced somewhat by your decrees and prayers and some minor activities engaged in randomly.

In short, it is time to take stock and to refocus and rededicate yourself, so that you might move most successfully to the next level.

You have been noticing that you are spending a certain amount of time in anger and resentment. This has been accompanied with judgmental thoughts of yourself and others and the attempt to drown it all out with reading or computer games. By suppressing them, they do not go away, but all too often emerge in little outbursts. Let us begin to address this directly. Yes, you are being tested. Yes, these thoughts are not all your own. And, yes, it is time to deal with them with the tools you already have.

We would point out to you that you have been avoiding looking at this, because you fear that underneath it all, you really are hopelessly contaminated and completely unworthy. We will address this first.

We will begin with a short guided visualization to take a look at what is truly troubling you.

Exercise 3:1-2 Sending Love to Heal

Beloved. Be at Peace. Bathe in the Love of the Creator. Feel the love soaking into the hidden recesses of body, mind and spirit. Where there is pain, invite yourself to relax more deeply and see and feel the Love moving into the places of pain and contraction. As the Love infuses this space, allow yourself to relax more deeply still.

*Let us look at the places where you are noticing pain. First look at your neck. Let the cells and atoms **ground** into the Earth. Let the muscles, ligaments, bones, nerves and all fibers and fluids ground as well.*

Draw on the Earth energies. Choose a copper and emerald green light to move back up the grounding cords and infuse each location with the healing energies of Mother Earth. Feel you body drawing up exactly the minerals and nutrients that will align you with ever better health. Allow yourself to remember to drink more water.

With whom do you need to communicate more honestly? What have you been afraid to really talk about? It is not the house. It is about feeling like the relationship is not serving you both. Do you feel that you are able to accomplish all that you desire? Do you feel supported and appreciated? Do you think that you might be complete for the time being? Do you think that you are both being triggered to see and to acknowledge areas where healing needs to take place? Can you love the part of yourself that needs this healing? Can you love and appreciate the other who is bringing this to your attention?

Now, close your eyes and imagine sharing what needs to be shared. Speaking what needs to be said and heard. And allow the healing to proceed exactly as is needed.

CR80

The next issue to be dealt with is loss, grief and abandonment. You have created a very strong shield around yourself to protect yourself from your feelings. You can remember your childhood when you cried yourself to sleep every day in despair. At the end of a year of this, at about age five, you made an intense life decision, "I am really very unhappy." This became one of the ruling features of your emotional life for the next 45 years, until you remembered it and cleared it. What you did not clear at that time was the buried and blocked feelings.

It is time now to go on a treasure hunt. For the feelings are, in fact, hidden treasures. They are the keys to emotional and material success.

Perhaps we will go a bit further back than this lifetime. Let us go to your lifetime as a pirate. Here again was a lifetime when both treasure and feelings were buried. So know that each unearthed feeling will be connected to treasure. Perhaps you can imagine yourself as the captain of your crew. You take a few select companions to help to row to the island and to dig the hole in which the chests are to be buried. Most of your treasure you yourself recovered and distributed fairly to the crew. But the last trove remained buried after your – shall we say untimely – death.

Exercise 3:1-3 Visualization to Restore Inner Innocence

Imagine yourself in full pirate turnout, coming to find not the physical buried treasure but the emotional one. Imagine yourself sailing through a storm-tossed sea. The ship fights the waves and the wind as you make for your target. The ship is blown off course, and you must sail many extra weeks to find the right location.

Finally, fighting a rough surf, you make your way to the island. Immediately you feel a sense of safety in this calm and peaceful spot filled with lush beauty as your feet touch the sand and wade to the shore dragging your small boat and beaching it high above the waves. The palm trees sway gently overhead.

Orchids are anchored throughout the undergrowth and colorful birds fly about the trees. Sit for a moment and let this moment of beauty and promise heal and soothe your battered heart and soul. It is time now to remove your rough and dirty clothing and step into a small pool near the beach. A beautiful waterfall drops down a high green cliff into this pool, and it is surrounded by low-growing plants and flowers.

This is the first memory that is to be purged. For on a very similar island, you once plundered and pillaged, raping the women, killing the natives and destroying the stone they worshipped as their god. This left a deep residue in your bones, your very cells and atoms carried the distortion of this action.

Stand now under the waterfall and let the water pu-rify, cleanse and heal every cell and atom of your body and your soul. Allow the weight of all dark deeds from every lifetime to be lifted away now through the gift of the Angels who have waited patiently for this moment. As these weights are removed, the distortions in your etheric grids can now be corrected.

*Step forward, away from the waterfall, and allow gentle hands to correct each bent and broken portion. All is swiftly restored to its original perfection. Indeed, new hands bring additional gifts and graces to the original **grid structure** and it shines more brightly still. As this process is completed, you may step out of the water onto the sandy edge of the pool. Here angels give you clean white clothing and lead you carefully forward to a small sandy spot under a large palm tree.*

A shovel is here and you take it up and dig where you are directed. You have to go much deeper than you antici-pated. And soon you find yourself standing at the bottom of a very large hole. Further digging reveals a door on your right. As you clear away the final mounds of sand which block the door, you reach out to open it and find that it is locked.

Your first instinct is to attack the door with the shovel, but the angels quietly shake their heads urging you to think of another way. You search nearby, but there is no key. You sit and spend a moment in silent meditation and then reach into a pocket you hadn't noticed before and find a key. This fits the lock and the door swings open.

It is very dark and dank inside. You are taken aback. Do you really want to enter when you are now so clean, even after all the digging. Yes, you assure yourself, this is my next step. I must go in and deal with whatever is inside.

You notice a small lamp just inside the door, and it is swiftly lit, shining light into the distant corners of the room.

Now, you are able to see that there is a long tunnel that extends further back, so you begin to explore this. The walls are dirt and water drips down them, but they appear safe enough and you continue.

By now, the pure white garments are getting quite dirty, but you know you must go on. The tunnel seems to continue for a long time. There are rooms to each side, but they are empty. You begin to wonder if there is really anything still here to find. But a feeling to go on keeps you moving forward.

Finally, you hear a faint sound. The tunnel curves to the right and the sound seems to get louder. It is the sound of crying. At last you approach another door that is closed. This is what you have been looking for. The door is barred on the outside, but it is easy enough to lift the bar and the door swings open.

Inside on a pile of dirty straw sits a very dirty and unhappy child. She looks up at you with surprise upon her tear-streaked face, because she thought no one would ever come for her here. Was she not abandoned forever? She is both hopeful and frightened. Who are you? Will you hurt her or help her?

You give a last thought to the white clothing and abandon all hope of getting them clean again as you move to gather the child into your arms and pick her up. "Come," you say, "it is time to get you out of here and back into the sunshine."

The child is still a little nervous, but after waiting so long, she lets hope win over fear and wraps her arms around your neck as you carry her back up the long tunnel.

You linger for a bit in the last room to let your eyes adjust to more light. And now the child wriggles to get down and she takes your hand and you both walk out again into the sunlight.

You take her with you back to the small pool. Removing dirty clothing, you both enter the pool and laugh and splash in the dappled water until hands and feet, face and hair are clean again. When you are complete here in the cleansing pool, you notice angels again standing on the banks carrying clean, dry towels.

As you emerge you are wrapped in warmth and toweled dry. Your clothing is once again snowy white and the child's rags have been replaced with a lovely, simple dress that would suit a fairy as well as a little girl. She twirls and holds her arms out wide and then pats at it, enjoying the feel and the movement and the color. She seems reborn as the sun shining through the trees lightly touches her shining hair and warms her skin. A soft glow seems to surround her and a shy smile touches her lips.

Who is this child? She is your inner innocence, your feeling body. Love and attention will complete her healing. Her delight in the world around her will bring new joy and love into your life as well.

And now, allow your attention to fully return to present time, bringing this innocence and joy back with you. For that which was lost is now found, returned safely to loving arms.

(Again, I remind you, while these exercises sometimes refer to various moments in Mikaelah's present and past lives, it serves as well for everyone. Modify the images or references as needed to make it more personal as you desire.)

Chapter 2

Healing the Emotional Body

Blessed One, we will continue with healing the emotional body. Today we will deal with physical traumas that left emotional residues.

One of the biggest physical traumas one can have is that which causes loss of consciousness or having the breath knocked out of you. This occurred when you were a young girl and fell off the horse and could not breathe for a few long moments. This was symbolic. The horse represents your power. Falling represents misuse of power or loss of power and loss of a level or levels of consciousness. Losing the breath refers to the disconnect from God.

We will start with the *Present Time Wand*.

Exercise 3:2-1: **Healing with Present Time Wand**

Recall that moment of traumatic loss of breath, and gently tap the part of your auric field where the memory is held.

Tap also the physical body at the solar plexus where the trauma was held. Now reach out to the levels of soul and gently tap the soul to clear any soul trauma that was related to this event in this lifetime and which also had links to several other lifetimes.

Tap the soul at the level of the third eye. Set your intention to clear, cleanse and heal every record, memory, pattern and trace of every cell and atom and particle at every level of consciousness, and in all times, all dimensions

94

and all parallel realities, worlds and universes. If you notice any part of your body holding tension, pain or darkness, tap there as well. Tap until all feels clear.

Notice any messages that may come to you and write them down if you wish to review them later. When you are in the slightly altered state of consciousness that allows you to work so deeply, you may not clearly remember all when you return to your everyday reality.

If you noticed tension around the throat or neck, clear this as well, because there were a number of lifetimes when the breath was severed permanently through a variety of deaths linked directly to the neck.

Next we will deal with traumas to the physical body that are related to being beaten or abused as a child or adult. To be caught in a situation where one may suffer at the hands of a bully, a parent or caregiver, a spouse or even a total stranger, sometimes repeatedly, is a terrifying and enraging circumstance. The physical body may mend, but the emotional body, the mental body and the soul often hold records that are not so easily corrected.

What beliefs do you begin to tell yourself? That you are unworthy, that you must be a terrible person to deserve this, that the world is not a safe place, that gentleness is a weakness. There are many variations possible here.

*Let us use the **Present Time Wand** to first tap the mind to heal both the memories and the false beliefs that were es-tablished. Some of the beliefs may connect to larger thought forms that were built up by many others, sometimes there are certain beliefs or patterns held within a family or a community.*

Other false beliefs might be held by whole countries or races or religions.

*Use the etheric **Sword of Archangel Michael** (It is a sword of Truth.) to cut any cords connected to false beliefs and then touch the energy field of the thought forms to dissolve and return to the Void the essential energies that created them.*

Let us turn now to traumas related to participation in wars of any sort – between tribes, gangs, belief systems (as in the Civil War in the U.S.), religious groups, countries, or even worlds.

There are many traumas to body, mind and spirit during a war. There are damages both temporary or permanent to the physical body. Wounds, loss of limbs, damages to sight and hearing, harm to internal organs and/or the nervous system. All produce a residue that can last lifetimes.

The shock of watching others slaughtered or injured is also traumatic. Observing the destruction of towns, farms, homes, and all the aftermath of war is also traumatic. The mind seeks to shut out the memories and the feelings but there are often nightmares for decades or crossing over lifetimes, after even one such experience, not to mention a lifetime or even several lifetimes.

୧୫

There may be a resistance to clearing any or all of this trauma, related to the belief that one must remember in order to honor the dead; never be tempted to repeat such an experience; strengthen the will to so act as to never cause such harm again, etc. These are in themselves false beliefs.

One does not have to remember ugliness to appreciate beauty. One does not have to remember death to honor the living. And so on.

Rather, one can choose to be fully present to beauty, to life, to the good however it presents itself. One can remember those who have passed on to other experiences in other worlds or fields of consciousness, without dwelling on the pain of loss. The value of negatives of any sort in appreciating the positive are part of the error, which is inherent in duality, especially that which was created for the lessons of the fruit of the tree of knowledge of good and evil.

The fullness of this understanding will emerge as the elevated consciousness of the New Golden Age matures.

Chapter 3

Dealing with Challenges

Blessed One, you are troubled that those you love will not be able to deal with the challenges facing them. You worry that your assistance will not be sufficient, that somehow they will be harmed.

Yes, the physical plane has held many challenges for those who abide here. And there are, of course, many opportunities as well.

When your children were babies, you realized that you could not watch over them every second. This was when you asked God to watch over them for you. This saved you from many worries, especially when you saw that they were protected from many dangers over the years.

Now, we ask that you again release those you love and watch over to the protection and guidance of their own **Beloved I Am Presence**. For no matter how much we love another and wish to provide every help, they are under the guidance and protection of their own God Self and specially assigned angels, guides and teachers.

You, on the same plane of awareness, cannot do everything. Nor do you need to. Yes, pray for all who are in need. Yes, share love, wisdom and healing with them as you are able. But do remember that each must walk their own path.

The chick cannot be helped from the egg or it will not be fully strong enough to survive. Even if you have forged a path that you feel would be so helpful and beneficial to them, still they must find their own directions, learn their own lessons, be true to their own knowingness. In short, you must let them be themselves and go their own ways.

Because these times appear to be increasingly challenging, some may wonder if things will ever ease up. We offer this prayer for these times.

Prayer for Help with Life's Challenges

Beloved Mother/Father God,
All That Is and beyond,
Be with us and all those we love
and care for.
Watch over and guide us each step
of our journey.

Be especially watchful
of the hearts and minds
that are being asked to grow beyond
all limiting beliefs.

Bring Faith and Trust to those
whose paths are not yet clear.
Bring Hope and Joy to those who struggle.

Bring rest and recuperation to those who are
striving to go beyond their normal strengths.
May your Love fill the places that
Have been emptied of the old ways.
May new Wisdom expand the vision
and the beliefs leading to new solutions
to old problems.

May each drink daily of Courage
to face life's challenges.
May Beauty touch each heart and
mind to inspire and uplift.

99

May all your precious gifts light the way,
ease the burdens, and fill
all hearts with gladness.

May each one see the ways
in which false beliefs and expectations
have created prisons of limitation.
And may they walk through those walls
into a world of greater Freedom,
greater Health, greater Prosperity and
greater Peace, Joy, Love and Wisdom.

May this time of rededication and
redirection be one of daily
increasing wonder and delight.

Thank you especially for the gift
of the *Violet Flame,* which we can
consciously wield, as we Forgive
and Transmute past errors
and present negativity.

Thank you for protection and
guidance each step of this path
into the New Golden Age.

Thank you for Healing,
Resurrection and Ascension
into the next level of Being.

We bless and give thanks for those
who have touched our lives
and gone on before us.

We give thanks for those we have not
yet met, who are still to come to bring us
new joys and blessings.

We thank you for the simple and
complex wonders of every
moment of our lives.

Thank you for the gifts you have given us
that we may share with others,
as we grow in Love, in Wisdom,
and in inner Strength.

Thank you for your Presence and
your watchful care in every moment
for all souls.
Thank you for Life.

So, beloved ones, focus on the gifts you have been
given, the blessings that surround you as you move through
these days. You are infinitely watched over, infinitely loved
and all is well.

I Am Jesus, and I hold each of you
in my Sacred Heart.
Know my Love and be at Peace.

Chapter 4

Traumatic Experiences

Blessed Ones, we will continue now where we left off on Chapter 3. For there is still much that must be dealt with regarding traumatic experiences.

We will start with traumatic loss of life of one who is dearly loved. This creates a shock to the entire system – physical, emotional, mental and spiritual bodies are affected.

How can we correct this? Which tools – indeed which miracles – can effect such a healing of body, mind and spirit? Is it even appropriate to undo such a huge life lesson?

First of all, we do not propose undoing a life lesson. What we propose is the healing of damage done to the etheric grid structures. We offer a healing of the mind and the soul, indeed of the planetary field itself, because such death affects all life on Earth. Because Earth has sustained such traumas billions of times over millennia, there is a huge clearing that needs to be accomplished in the etheric records.

We will start, however, with the individual, because the microcosm is the *template* for the macrocosm. Just as individual traumas affect the whole; that which affects the individual for healing also affects the whole. And at this time maximum assistance is being given for this healing.[9]

---

9   *We refer you here to several sections in Mikaelah's earlier book, **Live in Love**. Both the section on the core issues (pp. 32-34) and the section on damage to the etheric structures on Earth (pp. 175-177) are appropriate to review here. Both the text and the graphics are relevant to this discussion.*

We wish you to pause in this process for a moment and set your intention and expectation that such a huge and dramatic wound can be healed. We remind you of one of the lessons from *A Course in Miracles,* "There is no order of difficulty in a miracle."

"There is no order of difficulty in a miracle."

Indeed that is what is happening today in the realm of healing. Miracles of healing are happening every day. We ask you to believe that you can receive and participate in creating miracles.

Miracles: We assure you that it is time, now, to dissolve the beliefs that limit this Divine Gift. I once said that you would do greater things than I had done. If ever you believed that I spoke the truth, believe in this. Your destiny is to achieve greater and greater expressions of God/Goddess on Earth, and this definitely includes what you now call miracles.

ᨠᨮ

Exercise 3:4-1: Healing your Miracle Template

*So let us first heal the **template** in your etheric grids that allow you to create miracles. We remind you that miracles are an alignment between yourself, your will, and the larger whole, Divine Will. It is not about forcing your imperfectly understood will on reality. It is about knowing that God's will is perfection. This perfection extends to the health of body, mind and spirit and the correcting of any distortion or damage that has ever occurred, either in this lifetime or another.*

Miracles are an expression of Perfect Love. So let us start with an image of self – a holographic projection, if you will – in front of you.

All that you can accomplish in your mind's eye, will be accomplished for the whole.

It is not necessary or even desirable to focus on that which needs to be corrected, rather, know that your intention will focus the healing miracles into the exact perfect area in exactly the perfect way.

So, we call on the Angels of Miracles to come to you now. Let them rearrange and restore to perfection your own Miracle Grids. These templates in the etheric patterns allow you to co-create with God all miracles that are aligned with Divine Will for the greatest good for all.

Let there be healing and recalibration, now, in your belief that you are worthy and ready to receive this gift and to offer it to others. Let there be healing, now, in your ability to believe that it is time, and you are one with me, Jesus the Christ, and able and willing to so touch others' lives for the good of all.

Call on the Grace and the Presence of the Holy Spirit to bless you and to fully and completely anchor this gift into your entire grid structure.

*See and feel and know that you are the Christ of God – the anointed One – now here on Earth. See and feel and know that all of your four lower bodies are linked with, and fully aligned with, the Fifth Dimensional **Divine Blueprint of your perfection.***

Release now all resistance to the Light and Love now flooding your body, mind and spirit. Any dark or stuck places are allowed to relax and open and fully receive this light. Every cell and atom, every bone, muscle and organ, all fluids, every particle that is a part of what you know as "you" is now blessed and restored to perfect health, perfect peace, perfect love. Allow yourself to accept that it is so done now!

See the planetary grid, and see yourself as a bridge of Living Light linking from your location on Earth into the higher dimensional structures.

*Now, from a place of complete alignment with your own Holy Christ Self and the Oneness of All Life, call for the complete healing of all trauma in your own personal physical and energy bodies. Use the **present time wand** to tap any memories or particular places on your physical form allowing you to release any energies stuck in the past (either remote or recent) and to restore them to you in present time, fully cleared, cleansed and healed. Know that this is done in perfect grace and harmony for you, and that you will receive and assimilate these energies at the pace that is right for you.*

*Now take the Fifth Dimensional **Present Time Wand** and tap the Earth so that any healing might be replicated and multiplied for the entire planetary field.*

Planetary Healing

We ask that you come together in groups to hold an intention for healing miracles around the planet. For it is in the collective consciousness of Oneness that such large-scale effects must be created. Align yourselves first with me, Jesus the Christ, and then with the entire collective Christ

105

consciousness for the Earth, as you direct your intentions for healing and blessing the planet.

The new planetary grids for wholeness are in place in the Fifth Dimension. They must be anchored through you as conscious co-creators into and through the Fourth, the Third, the Second and the First Dimensions. This work will accomplish that around the Earth.

Exercises 3: 4-2: Working with the Unified field

Setting the field: *Let each one link with their own I Am Presence and feel that Presence fully resonant within them. Anchor that Presence fully into the physical body. Call on the Angels and Ascended Masters and other Divine Beings to be present with you and to join in your intention for the Highest Good.*

Each one sends an etheric link from heart to heart around your group.

The, each creats a heart link with the overlighting Group Presence (centered above your group) and with the Heart of Mother Earth beneath your feet, and so create a **Sacred Merkaba and Field of Oneness.** *Ask that it be filled with all Divine blessings and graces for this work.*

Ask and command that you, your group and the entire space be surrounded and protected with successive fields of white light, blue light and violet flame. Ask and command that there be angels set to hold the field and complete protection for all that you do.

Set your intention: *Speak your intention that you group be linked into the Fifth Dimensional Christ Grid and that you be connected with all other groups of like purpose.*

At this point you may focus your intention on a specific purpose, or ask that whatever is the highest order need might be served. You might wish to sit in group silence for 20-30 minutes. This might be followed by a time of conscious communion with one another and the Light and Graces that still fill the room.

If there is more to be accomplished in this phase, allow each one to speak, dance, share music or some other gift of spirit, as directed by their inner guidance.

Closing the field: *When the group feels complete, choose a closing ceremony that includes gratitude to all who have shared their light, their love and their wisdom and blessings with your group. When group process leads to significant raising of the energetic fields of individuals and the group, spend a moment to release all that no longer serves you and clear and transmute with the **Violet Flame**, in order to best sustain and integrate the new levels of light, love and consciousness that are the direct result of the shared work.*

If the pattern for the group needs to evolve, let it be done as Divinely guided and as Grace directs it.

Guidelines and suggestions for this work can also be found on **www.counciloflight.4t.com.**

Chapter 5

7th Dimensional Miracle Wand

Blessed One, we will continue to dealwith the deepest core issues. The subject of worthiness has come up. We will begin there as it is deeply necessary to healing of all other issues.

You know that you are worthy, because you know that God created you exactly as She/He intended. Yet, you have been programmed to believe that, somehow, you could undo God's plan through your own efforts and errors. Indeed, this is not so. But let us spend a few moments in something other than mental exercises, because that does not get to the emotional /spiritual core of this belief.

Rather, we are giving you a new tool here. Think of it as a 7th dimensional *Miracle Wand* that will allow you to tap distorted thoughts and beliefs lodged in your electronic bodies so that you might be restored to perfect form and perfect function on all levels, up to and including the 7th dimension, quickly, effortlessly and completely.

This will work on all false beliefs – the beliefs that you are damaged goods, that you are unable to help yourself, that you are intrinsically flawed, that you have a broken heart, that you are unloved and unlovable, that you deserve pain and suffering, that you are alone and abandoned, and so on.

Exercise 3: 5-1: **The 7th Dimensional Miracle Wand**

See me, Jesus, handing you this wand. See us together stepping into a beautiful garden setting where this sacred work can proceed. Know that I am with you, and that you have the power and the authority to receive and accept this healing for yourself and to share it with others.

Set aside just a bit of time each day to clear whatever comes up. Know that as you clear these mistaken beliefs, you are making a place for new higher order beliefs to be established in your consciousness and your etheric structures.

This wand will clear all energies of distortion including curses, hexes, spells, etc. that have been placed in your energy body. Negative extra-terrestial influences will be dissolved. Cords and any negative beliefs that allow them will be removed and health and wholeness restored. Memories associated with traumas that have affected you at the higher levels of soul will be healed.

The Miracle Wand will allow you to clear negative energies and entities from your home, vehicles and other personal spaces.

We will close for now, as this is deep work. Continue to work on whatever comes up for 20-30 minutes.

Chapter 6

Resurrection

Beloved One, today we will work with the feelings and beliefs generated through death, loss and destruction.

There is, within the core of man, that element of surprise that is still ignited when a friend or loved one is killed in unexpected ways. When death is sudden and violent, the element of disbelief is so strong that the entire energy body of the being is rattled.

This is also the shock that happens on a lesser scale when other forms of loss and destruction happen – such as a home being burglarized, especially when there is wanton damage, or when whole communities are damaged or destroyed through fire, earthquake, tornado, floods or hurricanes.

We would address the healing correction that is needed after such an event. The most important belief that is traumatized is the sense of essential safety and trust that life as we know it will remain in the same familiar patterns.

Sentient beings grow patterns of connection with other people, with pets, with familiar things, and with their sense of the community where they live. When these patterns are abruptly shattered, a person's sense of self, of who he/she is in the larger whole is intrinsically changed.

The power of prayer

This is where the power of prayer, which generates a resonant field, which is soothing and reconnective with that larger whole which is eternal and not subject to damage and change, is so extremely important. It is this power that has bonded people to their religious beliefs and to the sense of community and wholeness that is held there.

The **Sixth Ray** of Resurrection, Harmony out of conflict, Devotion and Selfless Service, is ruby and gold, and on some levels it is royal purple and gold. This energy can be invoked with the simple decree, "I Am the Resurrection and the Life".

For more about the Rays, explore **www.sevenray.net/ sri_education_introaw_sevenrays.html**. Other important books include: **The Seven Sacred Flames** by Aurelia Louise Jones, **The Rays and the Initiations** by Alice Bailey and others as you are guided, including the work of Patricia Cota Robles and Kamala Julianne Everett who work with the information of the 12 Solar Rays.

If you have an awakened inner vision, you can see the waves of resonant power that flow outward from the center of the one who speaks the words, "I Am the Resurrection and the Life" aloud.

"I Am the Resurrection and the Life"

This energy wave rebuilds whatever has been damaged or destroyed at new higher orders of strength, purity and perfection. It links the entire energy body, through each level of consciousness, into the higher dimensional patterns of both the personal and the planetary Christ grids of perfection – the Divine Blueprint. In so doing, it re-establishes and strengthens the sense of connection with the ineffable, with the Divine, which is the ultimate sense of safety and wholeness.

If you have healing needed in a particular part of the body, or even your life on a larger scale, you can say, "I Am the Resurrection and the Life of my feet. I am the Resurrection and the Life of my back. I am the Resurrection and the Life of my digestive system, of my first chakra, of my finances, of my family, of my nation", ...and so on.

It is possible to restore your physical body to wholeness in this way.

This is not to say that speaking these powerful words will bring back the old patterns that have been damaged or destroyed. It *will* allow you to be restored to a new place of harmony and connection with that which Is now. That which is gone will have a new place in your memory, but you will be, once more, at one with the pattern and flow of your life.

It is not needful to try, like Superman, to re-spin the world so that things can go back to the way they were. Change is inevitable. Growth is a constant. When you are in harmony with what is, you can come from the strongest, most healthy, and holiest – most whole – part of yourself to make the best choices, and align with the patterns and harmonies that are in greatest resonance with who you are and the next level of who you are designing yourself to be.

In certain circumstances of shock, it is not time to attempt to speak to the rational mind. Soothing at a non-verbal level is needed. Your intention for another for their ultimate highest good can be called upon.

Toning can be helpful to build harmony here, but not in such a way that it adds to the confusion or the fear that is already present. A quiet single note that is just barely audible to rebuild the harmonic connection is possible and appropriate and will not usually cause discomfort to anyone who might hear it.

The Harmonic Convergence

It was this resonating frequency of Harmony and Resurrection that was sounded in August 17-18 of 1987, during the two days of the Harmonic Convergence.

There were many circumstances which had happened in Earth's recent history which created a trauma needing to be healed. The explosion of the atomic bombs to end World War II was a particular world event clearly recognized as traumatic and shattering.

A second event which occurred, and continues to occur, was in the form of the new music of rock and roll. These patterns of sound were also breaking up the old patterns which had become so stuck and stagnant that life in all forms needed change.

But change, whether through war and destruction or sound and music, can be unsettling and disorienting. So, a wave that restored and rebuilt the patterns of life in new, stronger, healthier ways was called for.

Since the time of the Harmonic Convergence, the world and all life upon it have been rebuilding and repatterning into systematically higher and higher forms. The old forms that are out of synch with the new patterns are just not able to be sustained.

The patterns of Love that are being infused in and through all life insist on our releasing and dissolving all that no longer serves us. All that is not in resonance with the new frequencies, the new levels of conscious beingness, must be cleared, must be cleansed, must be either released, or brought to higher harmonic levels.

Thus, great waves of light, the divine qualities of the Creator, are infusing the patterns of Life on Earth and continuing to increase. Earth has entered a frequency band of light of increasing power and intensity. This time of transformation has been long expected.

When we willingly release all that is not aligned in harmonic resonance with the Light, we are lifted up easily

113

and gracefully. When we resist, the change happens anyway, but we experience pain and discomfort in the process.

We are releasing these concepts and these tools in this book to maximally assist this process for you.

We will close here for now. Thank you, dear one. All is well.

Chapter 7

The Chamber of the Sacred Heart

Dearest Ones of my Sacred Heart, during this time of transition, we ask that each of you place yourselves within the chamber of the Sacred Heart. Know that within this chamber, you are completely and perfectly guided and protected.

We offer you a short guided meditation in which to easily and effortlessly accomplish this.

Exercise 3: 7-1 **Chamber of the Sacred Heart**

Sit in a comfortable position with your feet flat on the floor. Allow your body to relax and center yourself in your heart. Breathe deeply and gently, and allow the breath to take you deeper. Drop your **grounding cord** *from the base of the spine into the center of the Earth and anchor yourself strongly here.*

Spend a moment calling for the full awareness of the Divine Presence that lives and moves and has its Being within you – your Higher Self.

Send love and appreciation to this Presence. Feel the Oneness that you truly are with this Presence and with All Life. Every cell and particle of Being is completely interconnected.

Breathe and follow the beat of your heart into the fullness of this pulsating knowing that you are One with All Life. The Life that flows through you with each breath, expands and flows into and throughout the interconnected Web of Life.

Breathe.

Move to the Heart of this pulsating knowingness. Feel a flow like the infinity symbol of a figure eight moving with the breath from your center to the center of the Great Sacred Heart.

Now, rather than feeling part out and part in, move all of your conscious awareness of yourself into the very center of this Sacred Heart. From this place, centered in the Heart of All that Is, you are in perfect resonance with all, and your every thought word and action now is in Harmony, Peace and Joy with All.

Breathe.

Repeat:

*I live and move and have my being,
centered in the Sacred Heart of All That Is.*

I Am in Harmony, Joy, and Peace with All.

I Am the Peace that passeth understanding.

I Am the Love that transfigures all.

*I Am the Wisdom which infuses Life
with perfect understanding.*

*I Am Health pulsating perfection into
every cell and atom.*

*I Am the perfect outpicturing of
my own Divine Plan.*

I Am in conscious Oneness with all life."

Remember who you are and place your attention always at your own center which is forever One with this Sacred Heart of All.

We are complete for today. All is well.

Chapter 8

Breathe in Peace

Stabilizing at the Present Level

For today, dear ones, we will be spending time realigning you and all of your energy bodies with Peace, Love and Healing, with your own Holy Christ Self, with your Divine Blueprint, and with the 12-strand DNA which is anchored primarily on the inner planes.

There is indeed more healing to be spoken of later, but for now, this balancing and harmonizing is needed before further progress can be made. You have been making HUGE strides toward your goal of health and wholeness. Today we are anchoring it more firmly in your field.

Exercise 3: 8-1: **Breathe in Peace**

So, once again, we ask you to focus on your breath.

In your mind's eye, see yourself sitting exactly where you are now. There is no need to imagine some ideal place. Perhaps you really are in a beautiful garden or quiet meditation place. Perhaps you are in a place that is beautiful, quiet and serene. Perhaps you are in a somewhat rumpled bed or in an office that is filled with things to do.

Wherever you are, it is perfect exactly as it is. Undoubtedly there are possibilities for improvement. Mikaelah's favorite definition of Heaven is: "In Heaven, everything is perfect. And there is still room for improvement."

Wherever you are, that is the perfect place in this moment. Do you have a series of unfulfilled desires? Let those thoughts rest for the moment. This now moment is taking place right here and right now in this location, however beautiful or ugly, pleasant or unpleasant. It is what it is.

Breathe in Peace to this place, this moment in time. There is no need to judge or evaluate. Breathe, and allow Peace to infuse you and to infuse this time and this space that you are experiencing. There will be time later for all the tasks that await you.

This moment, this Now, is for Peace. Feel yourself bathed in a column of Peace. Breathe it in. Bathe in Peace. Every cell and atom is filled with and surrounded with Peace. Repeat:

"I Am Peace.
Peace fills and surrounds me.
Peace is the Way.
I Am the Way.
I Am Peace."

Say it as often as you wish.

Now expand your vision of this column of Peace to include the entire space where you are right now.

Again Repeat:

"I Am Peace.
Peace fills and surrounds me.
Peace is the Way.
I Am the Way.
I Am Peace."

Again expand your vision to expand this column of Peace to include where you are in this moment and with each breath allow the expansion to enclose the entire community or region.

119

Repeat:

"I Am Peace.
Peace fills and surrounds me.
Peace is the Way.
I Am the Way.
I Am Peace."

And expand this to encompass your entire country,
continuing to breathe and repeat:

"I Am Peace.
Peace fills and surrounds me.
Peace is the Way.
I Am the Way.
I Am Peace."

And allow this column now to fully encompass the
Earth. Breathe and Repeat:

"I Am Peace.
Peace fills and surrounds me.
Peace is the Way.
I Am the Way.
I Am Peace."

From this place, all your true needs and desires will
be fulfilled in perfect grace and without effort. Repeat this
moment of full acceptance of the present. Repeat:

"I Am Peace.
Peace fills and surrounds me.
Peace is the Way.
I Am the Way.
I Am Peace."

Repeat this whenever you need to align yourself with
the Great Flow of the Tao, the way of Peace, the perfect
alignment with Grace and serendipity and all God's gifts.

*For the next several days, take time to walk in Peace.
Repeat the phrases. Look around you at your world and
gently repeat:*

> *"I Am Peace.
> Peace fills and surrounds me.
> Peace is the Way.
> I Am the Way.
> I Am Peace."*

We will briefly point out here that the mere process of aligning with the energies of Peace instantly and effortlessly aligns all the DNA within you with their highest and healthiest form and function, and all cells align with your Divine templates. All resonate with the greater whole, the greater Holiness of All Life.

Chapter 9

Seeing God/Goddess
in One Another

Blessed Children of the Light,

I Am with you Now.

I Am the Light of God which never fails.

You are the Light of God which never fails.

All proceeds in beautiful and miraculous ways.

Do you feel that only a miracle can salvage a particular situation?

Give thanks that it is God's Will that you deserve and shall have your miracles.

Dear Ones, it is the purpose and function of these books to assist you in resetting your beliefs and expectations toward that greater good which is the template of the New Golden Age. It is time Now for you to release ALL that no longer serves you in the newly emerging Fifth Dimensional realities.

We encourage you to once again return your attention to the breath. In the breath you are always in communion with God/Goddess. Allow the breath to be a place of Conscious Communion with the Allness that Is. Sit in the stillness and the quiet place of Peace within that is your center of Oneness.

Return to this place with increasing regularity and

frequency, dear ones. This is the place of synchronicity, serendipity and seeming miracles. This is the place where you recognize that Good is constantly being drawn to you to bring to you greater joy and peace. This is the place where you join with one another to co-create greater and greater good for All – through the breath, through your intention, through your attention.

Today we wish you to focus on seeing God/Goddess in one another.

When you begin to see and acknowledge and give thanks for the blessing that each one represents on Earth and in your life in particular, you are changing your view of the world.

As your view of the world expands to include the miracles that surround you daily – the wonders that are present in and through one another, you begin to believe and understand that you are also a miracle of Divine Presence and Divine Intention.

As you see God in one another, you also encourage them in their service and their work in the world.

Think of those you admire and love. Think of those who automatically lead you to think of Angels on Earth, Gods or Goddesses in form, fairies and leprechauns, and so much more.

All is hidden, dear ones, in plain sight. Begin to see with new eyes and to comprehend with new and more glorious understanding.

God is here now. God has never left you or anyone else. You were never abandoned, and neither were they. God/Goddess is in you and in all life. You are not alone and never were.

Every breath is God. Every pulsating particle of light or atom of existence is God expressing. God is in and expressing through everyone and every thing.

Everyone except those bad people or that bad mosquito, or those disease germs, or....?

No, everyone and everything is God expressing.

Then why do bad things happen?

Each person makes choices, dear ones, and God/Goddess has given humans the ability to choose freely. Some of the choices seem to be intrinsically bad: shooting children in schools, bombing innocent families during war time, diseases which destroy bodies and sometimes decimate whole societies, greed which clear cuts forests, destroys the environment, impoverishes one or many.

Sometimes the results of the choices seem horrendous and unforgivable, not to mention leading to results that may seem insurmountable.

Still, each person is returning over and over to choose again. In one of the Alice Bailey books dictated by Djwal Khul, it is said: "At first the lessons are between good and evil, and then between good and better, and then better and best."

The lessons are certainly ongoing, and just when you think you have gained some wisdom and understanding, the challenges seem to become more so.

It is not necessary to understand all the lessons, and all the choices, and indeed, where it is all going. What is necessary is that you send love, attention and appreciation to what you admire, and what you wish to see expand in your life and your world.

Remove your attention from what you wish to see diminish. You may call Angels to give assistance where there has been some personal, local or global disaster. You may call for Violet Flame to transmute any negativity in a given situation in the past, present or even the future. You may – you must – forgive, release and let go of the memories of past or present hurts. The only reason for placing your attention on the negative is to forgive, bless and heal.

The only reason for placing

your attention on the negative

is to forgive, bless and heal.

It is the act of forgiving and releasing that the next level of good can find space to arrive in your life and in the world.

And great good is pouring onto the planet at this time. Make it your mission to so clear, cleanse and heal yourself and your circumstances, that greater good can find space in your life. You then become a living template for good, for God's Grace on Earth.

Then, every person you meet, every place you go can align in Harmonic Resonance with the new, the good, the sacred. And so, Love, Harmony, Peace and Joy expand and expand, again and again.

Pain, suffering, disease and death diminish. Life, love, health and holiness increase.

Pain, suffering, disease and death diminish.

Life, love, health and holiness increase.

My jewel, my precious child, we are complete.

Chapter 10

Begin a New Cycle

Blessed One, we begin again, and we say unto you. Be at Peace. All is truly well. Those experiences that you most fear and reject are to become the cornerstone of your achievements, of your successful completion of these cycles.

So let today be the beginning of a new cycle on a higher round of achievement and glory in the realms of Divine Glory.

We start this day with praise to the Creator for each precious moment of life. Life is filled with ups and downs. Do you think that because a road goes up and down that you are making some kind of mistake? It is merely the nature of the road. Some roads are flat for a long way. These have their own kinds of problems. Other roads are very steep and filled with challenges. Still others roll along lesser climbs and gentler descents.

This is your life as well. There are times when the soul has no interest in the long, flat road or in the gentler ups and downs. The soul sometimes demands to be challenged. It needs to test its strength and prove its mettle in increasingly difficult circumstances.

This does not mean that you are a miserable failure. It means that life is rich and responds to all your needs and desires. When you start judging experiences while you are still in the midst of them, you can make yourself miserable. And, indeed, you can certainly extend that misery to those around you as well.

When you choose to allow the experiences to be what they are, and to accept the richness and the gifts that they hold, then truly you have learned to mine for gold and to find buried treasure.

Let us spend today, clearing away the debris of some of life's recent challenges. Have you been having less than harmonious relations with those around you? Has there been discord, strife or attempting to control things, each in their own way, with the end result of no one getting what was desired or desirable?

We could say "Into each life a little rain must fall." But that is not the issue. The issue is, are you being flooded by the rains, because you have not chosen to move to higher ground?

Let us take a look at what part of yourself desires to so control things that the highest choices seem to remain eternally elusive.

In Mikaelah's book *Live in Love*, there is a chapter on Sacred Relationships. It offered an extremely useful tool – ways of looking at different subpersonalities so that an individual might explore which aspect of him or herself was blocking a more successful and harmonious outcome. Which part perhaps needed further healing, or was interfering with those parts which could guide more successfully.

This extremely useful tool can be used again and again in a variety of circumstances. However, we wish to point out a different lesson about groups. It is that one cannot make a good group decision by oneself. All must be included in the process.

In the process of community building, this is key to building successful groups.

The Higher Selves of all must be engaged, and find a point of unity in the building and correct direction of a group. Even what seem like small decisions are steps toward building the larger whole.

So, when there is disharmony in a group, correct right action cannot be discerned by one person making the choices. All individuals must be aligned with their own Divine guidance in order to come to a correct group decision. Each one must be heard, and there can and will be a higher outcome that works for everyone, when all are choosing to listen to their highest inner direction.

Fear, control issues, and so forth do not lead to good decisions. Even the person who might seem to "get their own way" will be moved off course by such choices.

Those who are reading this chapter, have multiple life experiences that led them to these words. You already have the skills you need to sit as a group, to invoke your Higher Selves, and to set an intention to work toward successful decision making for all concerned. The exercise on p. 106 is an excellent way to set the field for all groups.

It is not necessary to spend a great deal of time discussing what isn't working, or to blame anyone or everyone for things that didn't work. If there has been discord, clear the energies. Clear that which is obvious and that which is subtle. That means that many more obvious problems have their roots in past life interactions. Clear all, clear all, clear all. Use the *Violet Flame, Ho'o Ponopono,* forgiveness in all forms. Then move straight to group consensus building.

Of course, each person has personal issues that they are working on. That is life. You didn't come here to float. You came to learn, to grow, to expand, to clean up the past and build new patterns for greater love, greater joy, greater harmony for yourself and all life.

If you are choosing to know greater love, to live a

more expanded and exalted life, to live in greater prosperity and abundance, clear out all that no longer serves you and build the new inner muscles, beliefs, habits and choices that will help you to achieve this.

Set your intention to achieve your goals. Each step will be guided. Allow yourself to listen and to follow your own knowing of Truth and Right Action. That will lead you forward. Is there fear? Acknowledge it. Focus your spiritual tools on healing the past, and choosing love in the present. Turn ever toward the light.

The challenges come from the habits of fear that have built up in the past. Let the Presence of Love surround you as you deal with what must be healed. Let Divine Wisdom lead you into new paths. There will continue to be new challenges, but let Light and Love and Power now restore the Plan on Earth. Or to put it in present time: Light and Love and Power *now* restore the Plan on Earth.

Another thought.

The Light of God always prevails.

The Light of God always prevails.

The Light of God always prevails.

And the Mighty I AM Presence is that Light.

May Light and Love and Power,
flow in and through you
according to God's Holy Plan
in the fulfilling of your Life's Purpose.

We are complete.

Chapter 11

You Were Created Perfect

Blessed and beloved One, all is well. Truly, all is well. You are so concerned for others, that you don't always take care of yourself. It is time for each one to stand alone and to know the power and the Presence of God personally. Some have been avoiding truly resting in the Divine Presence of God. Life has not handed them the kind of love and support they so desire, but even when surrounded by it, they have trouble accepting it. Challenges will arise so this can be dealt with. Each must go through this. Believe me, it is time – past time – for their spiritual progress.

Dear one, perhaps guilt has been running your life. Today we wish you to experience the alternative. You did not know that there was an alternative to guilt? Yes, it is your original innocence.

It is not just your innocence that we wish to address today, but that of everyone who has ever lived – every one, every lifetime, every planet, solar system, galaxy, etc. Purity and Innocence are your nature. Goodness, Truth and Love are your nature. Anything less than this is an error of thinking, feeling and believing.

You were created perfect. You are held perfect in the heart and mind of God.

What is this sense of imperfection then, and where does it come from? As part of the desire to know and understand what God is not, you created duality and separation. They are a construct based on an unreality.

It is time to resurrect the Truth of who you are in all times, all places, all realities.

At the beginning of this Book on Healing, we spoke of the nature of Health. Now we wish to speak of a greater Health and a greater fullness of Being that represents your True Nature.

Stay with me now as we explore the nature of God, and You, as a complete whole reflection of that. You have been guided many times in many ways to dwell on the true blessed qualities, the virtues, the pure templates of Being.

Exercise 3:11-1 **The True Nature of God**

Beloved One, Rest now. Rest in the true nature of God. Rest in the Power and the Presence of God. Rest in the Glory, the Light, the Love that God Is. See this as a sparkling, scintillating light in the center of your Being that touches every cell, atom, and particle of light that you are.

You are a pure and true reflection of God. Such a pure being is true, is holy. This comes into conflict with your idea of yourself as imperfect, as flawed, as filled with wrinkles or warts or bugs, bacteria, disease, deformities, sore spots, unhealthiness in any form. How can both be true?

Because you are creator beings with free will, you have the capability of creating and exploring even that which is not true. But dear ones, you, in the fullness of time, have decreed "enough is enough." This exploration of what is not true has no further usefulness to you.

You've explored it. You know more than you wish to know about that which is not true – the polarity of opposites. A whole world – yours – has been created in which you could explore this. And now, dear one, you are complete with this exploration. There is no need, no need whatsoever, to do a single additional thing here in exploring that which is not real, that which is not true.

*Oh, dear one, I hear, "My body is in discomfort. I'm
sneezing. My nose is dripping. There are discordant sounds
outside from the traffic. What can possibly be done to correct this?"*

*Hold the truth in your heart and in your mind. It has
been said, "The Truth shall set you free." The Truth that "I
Am a God Presence that is pure and true within myself,"
shall set you free. The first freedom is the freedom in your
consciousness, the freedom to let go of all that is false.*

*We invite you to release shame, guilt, false beliefs,
judgments of yourself, of another, of circumstances, of life
itself in this moment, so that you may know the fullness of
the Truth that you really are.*

*Every judgment is an attempt to find error in perfec-
tion – in God. That in itself is error. So let your final judgment be that judgment is no longer necessary. Judgment is
different from discernment. Discernment is the awareness of
that which is the highest and the best in any given moment.*

*Beloved, one. You must go deeper here. Come with me to
the depths of your being. To that place of blazing light pouring
forth endless splendor. See that light. It does indeed pour forth in
all directions. But there is a powerful Being that is directly before
you that is your path, your way, your truth, your life. Walk, walk
forward and see this Being blazing forth before you, before your
feet, each step, each moment – the right grace in tune with each
experience, indeed, each letting go, each self-correction.*

*Your body is now responding to this light which is
pouring forth. And you, as you shift on every level into this
light, this direction, this ancient wisdom of knowing right
action, all that you are is now aligning in perfection with
Truth, with Love, with all Goodness, all Health. Every sacred, precious, glorious, most wonderful Beingness is expressing now in you and through you.*

132

It is your Love, it is your Truth, it is your Heart that is sending forth this beam of Light. It is your feet that walk upon the path that is revealed. It is you who are the Son and Daughter – the Light of God – in form, in action on Earth. It is your Light that shines and opens a path that is so clear and so pure and so true, that other feet desire to walk this way.

Other beings are called to live in greater truth and greater love and greater joy and greater peace. Each being who walks this path of light opens the way for others who have similar issues, similar experiences that caused their own unique life story, and those things that require restoration into the divine perfection of the Immaculate Conception, the perfect blueprint of Being.

Walking one step at a time, in the Way, in the Light, in the Truth, in the Being – the pure Being Nature of God – allows that healing to encompass them. Their own nature resonates with Truth, with Love, with Beingness – and self-corrects.

Walk your Truth. Walk your Light. Walk your Love, and everyone is touched and assisted to also walk theirs. And soon all are walking in the Light, in the Truth, in the Love, and Great Glory is revealed. And perfect health is restored. Blessed ones, know the Light within you. Walk in the truth and power of that Light. That is God in you. Know that Light. Live in that Light. Let that Light express through you, fully and completely. You are the Light. You are the Truth. You are the perfect Divine expression in each step, each breath.

Each loving action reveals God's presence on Earth through you. You have come to be that Presence, that Love, that Grace in form. And you have taken on many distortions in this and many lifetimes. Not because that is your true nature, not because that is the reality of God, but because you have seen that there have been others caught in these errors.

133

Your Love called you to reveal the Truth, through your life, through your love, through your Presence – that God is real, Truth is real, Love is real and when reality is expressed, error and illusion cannot be sustained. Only the real is left.

Sit and hold this Truth, this Love, within you, within your heart, from head to toe, in every layer of your auric field, in every chakra. Let your body, mind and spirit, your feeling nature all bathe in the light of this Truth.

And we are complete.

Chapter 12

A Reminder

Dearest and most beloved one, be at Peace. All is well in the land of Oz. You are in danger of becoming overzealous. Did I not retire from time to time to contemplate, to meditate, to re-center myself?

You need this time of quiet right now. Let all be simple. Let all be peaceful. Walk in the Peace and Grace of your I Am Presence.

We will proceed tomorrow.

Chapter 13

Healing the Past

Blessed One, we are now ready to move on with this next chapter.

Let us speak of that young and playful part of yourself. For there is a part of each person which loves to explore, to play, to pretend.

This part of yourself is as important and as valid as the mature, sober-sided, adult portion.

In reality, each part and parcel of the complexity of being that make you "you" is valid and important. Some parts of this complex can have overlays of error which come from various traumas and dramas of this life, or earlier ones that are unresolved.

Let us address the needs of self to resolve and heal the past. This has been an ongoing process in this lifetime. You have chosen to complete these issues in order to move fully and completely into the higher frequencies of the Fifth Dimension, and as well, to bring a conscious memory of the errors of the past, so that superior choices might be made in the Now of each present moment.

There is a tendency when reviewing errors of the past to blame yourself, to judge yourself, to believe that you are intrinsically flawed somehow. (*We point out that you had a far more limited understanding of yourself and life in general in the past.*)

We ask you to clear this now in the following way.

Take the Fifth Dimensional **Present Time Wand** and tap each memory of past mistakes. Forgive yourself for those choices you have made in the past that you now can see and understand more clearly. Allow these lessons to be part of your maturation process.

When you were a young child, you made many mistakes. You spilled milk, perhaps were the cause of harm to a pet or a playmate, broke a lamp, etc. You do not hate yourself or blame yourself, because you know that you were just a child, and that is how children learn. See these younger aspects of yourself now in that light. You were a young soul in the midst of a learning process. Please forgive yourself – your many lifetimes and whatever errors ensued – now.

Exercise 3: 13-1: **Healing Self-Judgment**

*Call on the **Violet Flame** to transmute not only your past errors, karmas, etc., but also any past or present judgments you might have made about yourself.*

*Spend a moment looking at your body with your inner vision. Are you carrying burdens on your shoulders? Release them into the Violet Flame and into the hands of God and the angels. Is there accumulated weight on your body that is beyond what is needed and healthful? Tap it with the **present time wand**. Call on the Violet Flame to transmute the energy trapped in your body tissues. Tap your bones, your muscles, your fat, your blood, your nervous system, your skin.*

Tap areas where there have been injuries or where there is pain, disease or discomfort of any kind. Tap your heart, your lungs, your stomach, your intestines, your sexual organs, your glands, your kidneys, liver and spleen. Tap your eyes, ears, throat, mouth, teeth and tongue. Tap your hands and your feet, your knees, ankles, elbows and wrists, shoulders and hips, your arms and legs. Tap your neck, your throat, your head and hair. Tap your chest, back, buttocks and belly. Tap your spine from bottom to top or top to bottom. And send Violet Flame to completely transmute all energies that are released.

Send love and appreciation to your body, emotions, mind and spirit for all they contribute to the whole. Send love and appreciation to the whole that you are and the greater whole that is All that Is.

We will pause here. Spend time in silent contemplation for a short while. Find your place of balance and wholeness in this new clarity.

Chapter 14

The Divine Graces

Blessed child of light, there are so many concerns. Let us recommend one important thing at this time. Take care of your own needs at this time. You cannot be of assistance to others if you are not fully taking care of yourself.

Guilt, shame, blame and self-judgment are not serving you. Where do they reside in the body? Lies and deceit. Manipulation. Coercion. What behaviors of the third dimension must be completely cleared and released? How can this be done, and how does one person's clearing affect the whole world?

Worry, doubt, distrust, fears of all sorts – these are the energies now being released across the planet. In order to release them, each person must recognize that they are there, and then must choose new behaviors, thoughts and actions that do serve them.

Let us focus for a moment on those things that are serving each one on Earth. These are the Divine Graces that have always and do now serve us.

Focus on Faith, Trust, Hope, Love, Peace, Joy, Forgiveness, Health, Clarity, Harmony, and Wisdom. Focus on rainbow light, transcendent glory, the infinite beauty of the stars and the perfection of a flower. Focus on the gifts brought by trees. Focus on the delight of a smiling child, a playful kitten or charming puppy. Each moment brings a gift. Allow yourself to see the gift, to embrace it and to receive it fully.

Your every breath is a lesson in the present moment. With each breath you receive anew and release all that no longer serves you. You can always breathe more deeply, release more fully, find cleaner air, and so on, but we ask you to simply be aware that you already are practicing the perfection of giving and receiving, appreciation, and letting go every moment.

***Exercise 3: 14-1:* Clear what no longer serves you; Focus on what sustains you.**

So we will start in this now moment with a simple focus on the breath. Breathe in, breathe out. Inhale, exhale. It is already your most automatic and basic function. Whether you struggle or whether it is completely natural and effortless, your breath is a basic connection to oneness with the Divine and the great flow of life – the Tao if you will.

What are the stories that you tell yourself in your head? Is there a part of you that is constantly causing you to doubt yourself? Is there a voice that judges and condemns? Do worries about 'what if?' constantly consume you? You must first notice that this is happening, in order to address it and correct it. And notice the voices that support you and your vision for health, joy, peace and abundance. Choose to hear the voice of wisdom, love, self-esteem and sanity.

Take a moment to bring your awareness to the thoughts that no longer serve you, that cannot co-exist in the new energies that are infusing the planet. Allow your sacred breath to flow – in breath, out breath – and bathe the worries, doubts and fears in light, in truth, in wisdom and love. Watch as they dissolve and disappear as the illusions that they truly are.

Take the time to bring your awareness to the things that sustain you. In breath, out breath. Infuse them with light, with love, with power. Allow your consciousness to return regularly to this focus, and see them expanding each day, each moment.

It is your attention and intention that will expand what you desire, or diminish what you do not. Choose love. Choose life. Choose to align with your own highest knowing of Divine Purpose and Divine Right Action.

Say aloud:

I Choose Love. I Choose Life.

I Choose to align with my own highest knowing

of Divine Purpose and Divine Right Action.

There are so many suffering on this Earth. What is the nature of this suffering? This is the subject that the Buddha explored to its depth and it was at the core of his teachings.

Krishnamurti once stated, "Attachment is the soil in which the seed of sorrow grows." How can we love and appreciate each precious moment and still let go of all attachments?

These are questions to fill a lifetime of study and exploration. What can you do right now, in this moment with the understanding you already have? Deal with what is. Bring the focus and the understanding and the love that you already have to each moment, each choice, each decision, each thought and action.

Do the best that you can where you are with what you already have. If more is needed, it will be provided. When you are ready to receive more, you will see that it is already there waiting for you. Look at the world, your life, with the eyes of love and see all the gifts that are constantly coming to you. Give thanks now that what is needed is here now. Give thanks now, that you have the eyes to see it, the self-love to receive it, and the wisdom to use it well.

Ultimately, it is about love. Love yourself, love your neighbor, love your life, love God.

Dear One, Life is Love in action in you now. Trust now that I am with you in this and in all the experiences of your life. There is no separation that is real or true. That which is real is that we are all One.

Chapter 15

Embodying Your Divinity

Blessed One, set your priorities and proceed. If there is not a clear focus, then the work cannot proceed. This is an issue that you have to deal with, so we will address it now. Are you so engaged in self-sacrifice that you are not accomplishing that which you have come to do?

It is not the nature of the soul's mission to sacrifice itself and its purpose in order to "rescue" another. If there is not a true dedication to one's own soul truth, and the sharing of that gift of love and purpose that one has come to reveal, then the life has been misused.

In my case, I did indeed lay down my life, but it was to demonstrate a principle. The principle was that life is eternal, and that there are other levels of being that transcend death. It was not designed to teach people that their lives on Earth have less purpose than those on other realms. It was not to teach that death was to be sought as a way of service to others. The work that one is to accomplish on this realm cannot be done elsewhere, or you would not be here.

The healing and transformation that must be accomplished on Earth in the physical dimension is extremely important. Indeed, being here is a tremendous service to life. Each being on this planet is serving the greater whole. Each being is confronting those aspects of life and living that must be understood at the deepest levels.

It is not your job to suffer; it is your job to transmute both suffering and that which is the distortion of thought, word and action which has caused it.

I, Jesus, did not come to "suffer and die" but to transmit a teaching that would live beyond my human death. Each person who comes to Earth comes with a great soul purpose. Life on Earth can be tremendously challenging. And it is also the opportunity for tremendous soul growth, and the building of soul muscle and soul strength.

It is necessary to examine all beliefs that one has acquired during the course of a lifetime. Beliefs, habits, behaviors, family or tribal expectations – all must be evaluated and tested for their value, and whether they support or hinder one's life purpose.

You here on Earth at this particular time of transition into the next higher realm of being are being asked to examine all aspects of your life and to determine that which does and does not serve you. This is beyond the concept of non-attachment. The principle of life that you are serving at this time is that of the fullness of knowing your own True Nature.

When you know that you are expressing Divine Consciousness through your human form and human nature, there are things that must be done. To truly honor yourself as Divine, you must honor the gifts that you have been given and to search out all that is within you that is blocking or distorting the correct expression of these gifts.

That is why you have come to Earth. In honoring your soul's Truth you are creating new levels of Divine expression on Earth. You have not come just to be a great artist or author or designer of wonderful buildings, or builder of lovely gardens or grower of the healthiest plants. You have come to demonstrate Truth and Love and Beauty, according to the highest expression and highest understanding that you can achieve. This takes as many forms as there are individuals on the planet.

When you allow guilt or fear or any other error to block this, it is necessary to truly see what must be healed in order to move forward again. As each person confronts and transmutes their own personal "stuff", the entire planetary field is healed. It takes everyone working in their greatest integrity to accomplish the goals we hope and intend to achieve for the New Golden Age.

If there are those who seem to be working in direct opposition to these goals, see them as those who are highlighting that which is still to be accomplished. As the healing and transformation proceeds, the need to reflect negativity will continue to diminish and disappear.

While the world is still filled with that which requires correction, each individual has come to address only their particular portion. No one person needs to do "everything."

Each one has come with a particular array of gifts and abilities which allows them to accomplish their portion with maximum grace, ease and joy. Trying to do someone else's work will not lead to the highest accomplishment of the Divine Plan.

We are each called to do our own work. We are each called to grow and love and heal and serve in unique ways that work in harmony and lead to peace and joy for ourselves and the greater whole.

Each day there are new opportunities to clear, to cleanse, to heal, to share, to create, to love, to rejoice, to be at peace.

Each day there is the opportunity to grow in understanding of ways to be more closely aligned with the great goodness that is God. Each day there are greater opportunities to be that Presence in unique living embodiment. Each day there is the opportunity to anchor Heaven on Earth in greater and greater measure. This is why each of us has come to Earth at this time. This is the purpose of human embodiment. This is the soul's truth.

We have spoken of these things many times in many ways. The very statement "I Am the Way, the Truth and the Life" is an expression of the Divine in form acknowledging itself.

Let us close this discussion with a simple Truth. All life is God expressing. Honor God within yourself and see and honor it in one another.

Namaste.

Chapter 16

You Are the Gift

Beloved One, Oneness is what we are together in the Infinity of Being that is the All.

Blessed One, take a moment now to know that the Divine in you – the Divine in me – is a perfect reflection of the all. Just as a hologram can be broken into a million pieces and each is a perfect reflection of the original, so too is each being a reflection of the One.

You are concerned that you are not able to perfectly reflect that message that is being transmitted to you. Let us speak of your concern for a moment. It is virtually impossible for one person to perfectly transmit a communication from those of us on the inner planes. There are a number of reasons for this. We will enumerate them.

1) That which is being transmitted must go through the densities that still surround the Earth plane.

2) There is often interference from those who are seeking to stop these communications.

3) The individual who is receiving the transmission has their own issues which are being triggered by the mere fact of the higher vibrational frequencies of the transmission entering their consciousness.

4) Environmental factors at the time of transmission are a possible added interference.

5) Issues of heath may be an interfering factor.

6) There may be other persons in the environment whose thoughts and energy field are a disturbance or interference.

In spite of these and other less common factors, it is deemed important to continue to offer these messages in spite of the problems.

1) It has value for the individual who receives these transmissions in the raising of the general frequencies of their field and, as well, the purification and healing which is a direct consequence of this work.

2) In raising the frequency of the individual messenger, all those around them are also touched by this energy field, according to their own conscious or unconscious receptivity.

3) The planet itself is affected. The message which is received and its larger field of consciousness and intention is anchored thereby into the planetary mental body.

4) The ideas and concepts themselves touch those souls who are ready to receive them, and indeed, even those who will be ready in the future, assisting in their own transformation process.

5) The very process of willingness to work with those of us on the inner planes anchors blessings far beyond the actual words received and recorded. In choosing to serve the greater whole, there are actual corrections made in the larger mental body of the planet, which hold the errors which are the results of the misuse of humanity's free will over the course of millennia.

6) Those who sit in the field of a transmission, whether it be an audio recording, a book, an email, or in an audience, are receiving the wholeness of a transmis-

sion, not just the words as spoken or written. They are thus affected by far more than the obvious.

Thus, there is great value in the willingness to, and the actual receiving of these transmissions. As well, it is important to acknowledge and affirm this value, and to set an intention that all that is being accomplished be for the highest good for all concerned.

No one is asked to do more than their best.

Blessed one, all is well. Hold a vision of the larger picture, the great good that is being served, and acknowledge your own part in this. We are grateful to you and to all who receive our messages with love and joy and appreciation.

Blessings to you. We are complete for the moment.

Chapter 17

Clearing Karma

Blessed One, we wish to spend a moment speaking of the clearing of karma between beings at this time. In order for all to move on, these karmic records must be cleansed and transmuted.

Join with me now as we call for healing and blessing for all concerned in this matter.

There are times when that which has been between two or more people must be cleared through new choices and new behaviors between them in actual physical circumstances. At other times, it can be cleared on the inner planes.

Clearing on the inner planes can most easily be done with the use of the *Violet Flame* through decrees, intention and visualization. The *Ho'o Ponopono prayer* can also be used very effectively. Simply repeat the words with intention and attention focusing on one person at a time.

The Ho'o Ponopono Prayer

"I'm sorry. Please forgive me.

I love you. Thank you.

I release it."

When the darker energies have been invoked through curses, black magic, or the interference of negative extra terrestrial or other malign beings, then there might be a more extensive clearing required.

You may always call upon me, Jesus, to assist in these instances. Whether you have the tools or the experience to deal with such circumstances or not, I am willing and able to give you any assistance that might be needed. Merely call my name three times and I will come and give you the assistance that is required.

For example you might say:

"Beloved Jesus the Christ,

Beloved Jesus the Christ,

Beloved Jesus the Christ,"

and then add your specific request for my assistance.

It is our desire that you each have maximum assistance in this time of clearing, and as well, that you feel cleansed, empowered and uplifted in the process.

If the challenges that you are facing end up triggering doubt, fear, guilt, blame or other negative emotions, allow that it to be an opportunity for still deeper clearing. It is vital to bring all of your intention and your focus to what is being brought up to clear.

That which has captured your attention, is what needs to be dealt with. Honor yourself for the willingness and the courage to do so. If you are alive on the planet now, you have agreed to deal with as much as is possible for yourself and all life.

Now, we wish to speak to you of some of the ways that you might use the *7th Dimensional Miracle Wand*. First, envision that it is right in front of you. See it. Feel it. It may be used in multiple ways.

- It might be played like a flute to infuse musical patterns that will allow the correct resonating frequencies to be directed toward that which requires healing and transformation. You might tone in harmony with what is being played on the inner planes.

- You can use it to gently tap each vertebra from top to bottom or bottom to top. This is best done slowly and consciously from the tailbone on up. Pay attention to the effect at each step.

- The wand can be drawn down the energy meridians or down the arms or legs. Allow your mind to stay focused on your highest intention for health and wholeness for any part of the body that is experiencing, pain, dis-ease or discomfort.

- For body systems, such as the immune system, the blood-vascular system, the nervous system, the lymphatic system, etc. a certain amount of knowledge is useful, so that you might hold the whole in your field of intention. However, it is more important that your "eye be single," that is, that you maintain a clear, focused intention for health, as you tap and hold the wand on pertinent locations, allowing a flow of mighty cosmic power to be directed in and through the system.

- If there is a need for mental healing of any kind, focus the wand on the pituitary/pineal area of the brain, just above the nose at the center of the head, while holding your intention for the complete healing and clearing of any distorted thoughts or mental imbalances.

- For spiritual healing, hold the wand over the 7th chakra, and see the cosmic energies entering through the crown of the head and flowing through the entire chakra and meridian system, and then through each layer of the auric field.

- Planetary healing work is best done with a group. Let each one point their wand toward that portion of the earth needing assistance. This can include the physical, mental, emotional, social, political, economic

152

and spiritual arenas. Speak aloud the intention for the highest good for all concerned, that it might be achieved with maximum grace and ease.

- Clearing of karma to the maximum extent allowed by cosmic law can also be enhanced with the Miracle Wand.

- Focus the Wand on your heart. Set your intention for the maximum healing and clearing possible. Imagine that you are creating an energy flow from heart to heart in the form of a sidewise figure eight, an infinity symbol, between your heart and that of another person or persons involved in the karma. The flow will clear the field and restore all to alignment with the Divine Plan, allowing each to move forward more clearly in accomplishing their expression of Divine Presence on Earth through their individual uniqueness.

- It has already been mentioned that the Miracle Wand might be used to clear curses. (Chapter 5)

- For malign influences, tap the construct or being three times to restore harmony, grace and peace.

The Miracle Wand directs the energies of the *Tao*, the collective energies of creation. As we have described before, (See *Live in Love*, pp.133-136) the Tao can be perceived as a great flow, somewhat like a whirlwind. Those intentions which are clearest and free from repercussion (i.e., generating no karma) are in the still center of Perfect Peace, while those thoughts, words and actions which are not clear are further and further from the center, and generating more and more disturbance. A tornado is the best example on the physical plane of what this flow of the collective thoughts, words, choices and actions of all life looks like.

In choosing to work with the Miracle Wand, you are setting your intention to be a conscious co-creator with God/ Goddess/All that is. It is always wise to intend that all that

153

is accomplished be for the highest good for all concerned. Any particular blessing that you would like to direct to a particular person(s), place or thing is then always aligned with right action.

We are complete for today.

Chapter 18

The Gift of the Presence

My dearest love, be at Peace. We ask that whenever there is that which causes you dismay or concern, go immediately into the place of stillness within and call upon the Sacred Heart of God/Goddess/All That Is to enfold you and all that is disturbing to you. Bring your concerns for Self or others here and give them to God. Then let go and know that all is well.

For example, let us say that you are experiencing temporary discomfort in the physical body. By moving your consciousness to the Sacred Heart, you align your body, mind and spirit with Oneness, with the Divine Perfection of Being. This brings forth optimum health and well being. When you are concerned for another, your alignment with the Sacred Heart consciousness allows Divine Perfection for the optimum outcome to be established for all concerned.

If there is discord or disagreement between you and another, bring the whole subject and all those concerned into the Sacred Heart Consciousness to allow that which is the highest outcome to be made manifest.

Dear One, we say unto you, all is well. Please be constant and consistent in returning to this knowing – this understanding.

Each day there are new concerns to be addressed. Each moment is another opportunity to call the Presence of God into conscious communion with you, and to infuse your life with ever greater love, wisdom and divine purpose.

Allow yourself to be always ready to receive more joy, more gifts, more abundance on all levels. When you focus on the past or the future, you disconnect from the gifts of the present moment. (Did you notice that it is the Present moment? If you are not reading these words in English, "Gift" and "Present" each mean the same thing.)

It is only in the present that healing and transformation can take place. If you are caught up in the past or the future, you cannot be here.

Years ago, Mikaelah saw a beautiful poster from Australia. It said:

"My name is I Am, not I was, not I will be.
You will find me in the present.
Not in the past and not in the future."

So know your Presence in the present, and receive the gift/the present of the Presence that this represents.

It good to spend time in meditation with that Presence. Indeed, it is mandatory. That time of silence and contemplation and inner attunement improves your ability to bring that Presence into your daily waking life. And it is this full alignment with and conscious embodiment of the Divinity within that is the life goal of each human being.

When there are circumstances that cause you distress or concern, affirm your alignment with the Divine Essence within. Affirm your Oneness with good, with God. Bring problems or concerns to this Presence, and know that your intention to align with the highest good, places you in the flow of right thought, right opportunities and synchronicities, and right action, leading to right outcome.

We are complete for the moment.

Chapter 19

Prosperity

Blessed one, imagine if you will that your prosperity grids are directly related to your willingness to take care of yourself as well as others. All must be in balance in order for prosperity to flow. Be patient. All is well.

Today we will be speaking of prosperity because, in truth, health and wealth are in the same lineage, the same flow. Many have noticed that in seeking to restore health, wealth can flow quite dramatically in accomplishing this goal.

There are, in fact, two distinct personal grids or templates that are connected – one to physical health and one to financial condition. It is less well known that these grids are interconnected. So, to prosper the body's health, prospers the financial condition as well. Or vice versa, to prosper the financial condition, prospers health. These are general terms, and there are also specific karmic overlays that can certainly add to the mix and make the interconnection less obvious.

Certainly, it is well known that having an abundant income means access to better health care. Again, this is a general rather than a specific condition, as some health concerns do not have known cures.

But we digress.

Let us return to the concept of prosperity, which encompasses far more than health or wealth. Prosperity is linked to the flow between individuals. Let us speak of prosperity which blesses all. Let us explore and experience true prosperity as the great flow of the universal Tao. In true prosperity, each and every person, thing or condition which is useful or desirable flows to you without stress or effort. And all are blessed by these interconnections.

It has been said that the western form of meditation is business. It is here that extreme focus and concentration is developed. It has been through business that a certain form of prosperity has developed in the west. But there has been a distortion. Greed and insensitivity to the needs of the larger whole have created worldwide problems which now must be dealt with if all are to truly prosper.

The water, the air, many species, the earth itself – all are endangered. So true prosperity must encompass that which serves the greater whole. It is not that some have accumulated a greater proportion of worldly things than others. This is a reflection of the accumulation of spiritual merit or accomplishments of individual souls over eons of time as well as karmic lessons. It is not necessary that everyone have exactly the same amount of the same things; rather it is necessary that each one have according to their own purposes and needs.

What are the needs of the plants, the animals, the entire ecosystem for true prosperity to flourish? How can one truly understand the larger picture well enough to make the right decisions to begin with?

Certainly these are good questions. However, it is not necessary to know and understand every detail, in order to find that place within oneself of knowing and choosing right action.

Let us start with the idea of developing a simple garden on your property. This is something that Mikaelah has been doing and has already discovered some of the many factors that need to be considered. She had ideas of what could be accomplished and proceeded ahead to select an area, surround it with a fence, till the ground and plant both seeds and young plants. Then the idea came to raise chickens and a suitable area was selected and a small coop built. Chickens were acquired and it soon became evident that a significant learning curve was developing on space requirements, the degree to which chickens naturally dig up every plant in their area while looking for bugs, and so on and on. The weeds in the garden were flourishing, the plants somewhat less so. The chickens were a delight and tearing up everything in sight.

Then it became apparent that a major step in the process had been omitted. The Guardian Deva for the yard was not happy. The chickens were suddenly laying eggs in hidden spots all over the yard rather than in their nests in the coop. Plants that were growing well were suddenly being uprooted and trampled by the chickens.

What hadn't happened was cooperation with the local nature spirits, and communication of intention and desired outcome. In fact, in every endeavor, following the original intention or idea, must come alignment with the elemental kingdom, the builders of form. When this is in place, all the kingdoms can work in harmony toward the goal. This is the problem that exists across the Earth.

Most native societies have built up a working relationship with nature over millennia. In the West, the industrial growth of the last few centuries has disrupted this working relationship, and now the entire Earth is in danger, due to lack of awareness and limited thinking. Societies that had been working fairly effectively for centuries were being buried in so-called progress.

Did you think that the transformation into the new Golden Age was going to resolve these problems automatically? Well, that is not the case. If you wish to live in paradise on Earth, you must know and follow the rules.

Did you really think that recycling your water bottles and newspapers was a big enough change to help? It is necessary for an entire revolution in thinking to happen. And just because you have been doing your spiritual homework, doesn't mean that you are finished with your lessons here on Earth.

The Earth has demanded and received permission to cleanse any area where there is significant lack of respect for the needs of the whole. You may think of the earthquakes and tsunamis in Japan, the tornado in Oklahoma, the hurricanes in New Orleans and the East Coast of the United States, to name a few more recent examples. These have been significantly minimized to what might have happened, due to many prayers around the world.

But there is a great deal more that needs to happen and happen soon, if worse is to be avoided. Every organization and business on Earth must develop self-awareness and a sense of their larger responsibility to the Earth. Everything from banking, government, medicine, religion, education, law, farming and food production, transportation, manufacturing, the internet, zoos and wildlife preserves, and municipalities large and small, must step up to the plate. Profit is valuable in order to keep things going, but it can no longer be the primary rule of success.

Only those who successfully make this transition will survive the next level of change.

The elemental kingdom is key to making this transition successfully. Needless to say, those who do not see or believe that it even exists will be at a significant disadvantage. But there are examples of those who are making a difference through sheer intention and devotion to basic principles of right action in relationship to one another that demonstrate that it can be done. Mother Theresa set a good example of that.

Every community on Earth must address these issues or perish. The predominant motive must be the greater good of all. Amassing great wealth and power will not be any kind of protection at all.

We will be speaking of ways and means of addressing these issues in our next book.

We are complete for today.

Chapter 20

Prosperity Principles

Beloved One, we were speaking of true prosperity. The prayer you wrote to the Angel of Abundance[10] was a reflection of the principles.

Oh beloved Angel of Abundance,
I give thanks for all that I have received.
I open to receive anew
from the abundance of all life.
My prosperity blesses all.

Let us examine the principles revealed in the above prayer.

- Acknowledge that there are higher powers that influence our lives.

- Express gratitude for all things received, not just the obviously pleasant.

- Be open and receptive to the good that exists abundantly all around you.

- Know and act on the knowledge that sharing is key to the flow.

Acknowledgement: There are many levels of being-ness, and those in the higher realms may be called upon to give assistance according to their specific area of focus.

There are vast levels of study to learn more of the Angels, the Divine Rays, and those exalted Beings which express

---

10   Visit www.mcordeo.4t.com for a download of all the prayers for *the Heart of the Goddess Aromatherapy blends. Each prayer includes greatly synthesized spiritual truths and teachings.*

throughout the multiverse.

One doesn't need to know the names of every Angel, or call on Beings from all religions to receive help, however. Working with those who are familiar to you is sufficient in almost all cases. If there is ever any doubt or a wish to "double check" one with whom you are choosing to work, there is a simple rule of thumb –

If it doesn't come from Love,
it doesn't come from God.

More simple tools to check that you are not connecting with a being who is pretending to be the one you are calling on, include the following:

1. Use the sword of truth of Archangel Michael. Set your intention to reveal the truth. Point it at the being and an imposter will be revealed or disappear.

2. Ask if the being stands in the white light of the Christ, the violet flame of St. Germain or the gold light of the Buddha. Pay attention to the answer.

3. In the Bible, you are advised to test the spirits and told that by their fruits you shall know them. Be vigilant and examine yourself, your motives and your areas of growth that are being triggered by your experiences. Are you growing spiritually? Is there greater love, greater joy, greater health, greater wisdom that you are receiving and expressing?

Gratitude: The Bible says to give thanks in all things. This is a whole spiritual practice in itself.

It is said that gratitude must be practiced in order to successfully manifest. Undoubtedly there are many factors involved. However, we suggest to you that it will be worthwhile to spend some time examining gratitude.

How does it feel in your body? What happens within you when you decide to "feel grateful?" Do you feel a smile emerging? Do you feel lighter, more relaxed, more peaceful? What are the reactions you see in others when you express gratitude?

What happens when you choose to be grateful in more circumstances?

Mikaelah wishes to share an experience she had once in exploring forgiveness and gratitude. She had young children who had recently received new bikes. While they were behind a fence on the property, they were not locked up. One day, some roofers were working next door and clearly able to see the bikes. The bikes disappeared that night. Mikaelah decided to forgive rather than confront these probable thieves.

There was no visible change in her life, but Mikaelah noticed that she lived on a very busy street. The few blocks to school that the children might have been riding their bikes on were in fact a bit dangerous. Perhaps the nothing that had happened was in fact a bit of divine grace in a tragedy that didn't happen. She decided to be grateful that the children were watched over and protected in ways she didn't even know about.

Do you think that you might also be watched over and protected in ways you are not aware of? Perhaps you could be grateful for this? Indeed all life is filled with so much for which we can obviously be grateful, and even more that is hidden because of what didn't happen.

A fabulous and very simple meditation practice is to simply sit and spend a few minutes thinking of everything you are grateful for. And occasionally, you might wish to explore the practice of giving thanks for the other kinds of experiences – the not so obviously gratitude-inducing. What of the difficult experiences that brought beautiful life lessons? What of the unpleasant but necessary experiences in which karmic debts were completed? What of illnesses that forced you to examine and clear deep personal issues? How would your life be different if you saw everything as a gift? It's just a thought.

Open and receptive to good: That leads to the next principle. When we begin to see that life is constantly bringing opportunities for good to us, we are able to let go of our shields and our protections, and are able to be more open and ready to receive that which love is bringing to us every day, every moment. When all is perceived as good, we can know we are loved always. We can know that we are worthy of love and of all good.

Are there beliefs you have collected that you are not worthy enough, good enough, acceptable enough? Perhaps some subtle inner voice says you don't deserve the good things. Perhaps you could release these mistaken thoughts about yourself and create new ones that reflect your higher understanding of what is real, and what is true about yourself and about life. This is the process that is underway now as we step through the doorway into the Fifth Dimension.

Even beliefs that seem to be good can be limiting compared to the more expanded awareness that will be fully available to you in the Fifth Dimension. Do not be afraid to explore letting go of an old, limited Third Dimensional belief to experience what a more expanded belief might look like.

Perhaps it is time to explore your life choices in this regard. Marriage, work, relationships and agreements of all types will be understood in new ways. In what ways are you willing to let go of old patterns, so that new, higher order, more expanded, Fifth Dimensional ones might emerge?

Sharing: Some people are well versed in this principle. Some are not. A person who hoards is a person living in lack. There seems never to be enough. Life is felt to be fearful, dangerous, filled with possible loss.

Blessed One, Be at Peace. In the Peace that passeth understanding all needs are met. All doubts and fears are dissolved.

You are to feel and know that you are a wayshower for the planet. It is not necessary to see all those who are able to follow the energetic patterns that you have built. But it is necessary that you believe it, because believing that you have done very little is not serving you.

Trust that this path that you have forged on the inner planes is in fact serving millions. You have given hope and inspiration to many that you will never meet. All the fears that you have met and overcome, all the difficult choices that you have made, have left a trail that has made it easier for those who follow.

Today is a day for invoking and expressing hope, dear one. Meditate on hope at this time, for it is hope in the things which are yet to come which allows energy to flow toward the desired outcome.

It is Hope in the things which are yet to come

which allows energy to flow

toward the desired outcome.

There are many who feel hopeless. Their circumstances have felt impossible to correct. And yet, with God/Goddess, all things are possible. Let us say a prayer asking the Angels to bring hope and sustenance to those who are feeling overwhelmed by circumstances.

The Light of Hope

Dear Mother/Father God,

We ask that you shine the light of Hope
Into the hearts and minds of those
Who believe there is none.

Fill the darkness with light.
Inspire others who might
Give assistance to act
In small ways and large.

Let old patterns and beliefs
Built by doubt and fear be released.
Let Grace and Miracles
Shine unto each life.

Let your Strength, Courage
And Hope rebuild lives.
Let Light and Love and Power
Rebuild each life into the next level of being.

May all be reborn in Light,
And be renewed in Love,
May Earth regain her splendour
And all life rejoice in each holy day.

Chapter 21

Fear of Loss

This message came after I had received a long protocol on using the new Miracle Wand. It suddenly seemed to disappear from the computer. I was quite upset. However, in retrospect, I see that loss of anything creates its own traumas and dramas and opportunities for healing. So I am including it.

Dear One, there is no need to be dismayed that somehow you have lost anything. It is not true nor necessary to be worried that there is anything "missing." For now, let us say that the protocol information is not to be shared. That which it contains will be revealed at another time.

Now, you have seen the ways in which you tend to get caught up in self blame and self judgment when something does not go as you had expected or intended.

We say unto you, be at peace. Rather than searching for that which had been lost, your time would have been better spent in recreating it at the next higher level of being.

For now, let us say that was a lesson in itself in forgiveness and in looking at what needs to be healed.

Use the ***Present Time Wand*** to clear energy stuck in the past that prevents you from accomplishing your goals. Clear your office, your work, your books, your films, all is affected. Use the ***Miracle Wand*** now to clear your body, feelings, mind and spirit of all that is interfered with now or at any time in any reality. So be it.

All is well. Get on with your day.

Chapter 22

A New Protocol for the
7th Dimensional Miracle Wand

As I was completing the book and editing, this protocol appeared. I don't know if it was the original one or a new one. In either case, it felt like Divine Grace in action

Dear One,

I Am Jesus and I Am with you now and always.

When you wish to use the Miracle Wand, I wish to offer a simple protocol.

1. Set a sacred field of love, healing, safety and protection. Call on the Angels, call on those Divine Beings who work with you or the person(s) or circumstances that you wish to assist, call on those specific Holy Ones with whom you have the greatest love and affinity. Say:

   "I call on the Archangels and Archeai of all the Rays to come and hold this space sacred, holy and divinely protected. I call on my own I Am Presence and Holy Christ Self and that of all concerned. I call on Jesus the Christ, Mother Mary, Quan Yin, Krishna, Buddha... and I ask that this space be flooded with Violet Flame to clear any all possible negativity and that a sphere of cosmic white and gold light surround all with Divine Love, Wisdom, and Perfect Right Action."

2. State your intention for the Highest Good for all concerned.

*"May all that I (we) do
be for the highest good
for all concerned,
in full alignment with Divine Will."*

3. Accept and know that you are ready and worthy to call for and invoke miracles in your life. Say -

"I Am ready and worthy to claim a miracle."

4. Claim your willingness to serve as a conduit for God's Grace. Say -

*"I Am a willing conduit for
the Grace of God's Miracles now."*

5. Speak with Divine Authority as you call for Divine Grace to touch the situation and bring about God's healing miracles in the perfect way according to God's Will. For example:

- *"Clear all curses, hexes, vows, incantations or false beliefs connected to this circumstance now."*

- *"Clear all cords, bindings, devices or attachments now. Violet Flame/Burn them back to their source(s) and neutralize their source."*

- *"Clear, dissolve and cancel all vows, contracts, covenants, promises, agreements and/or false beliefs connected to this circumstance now."*

- *"Clear, dissolve and cancel any potential repetitions or linked curses, etc."*

- *"Light around any hidden or disguised energies or beings. Let them be revealed."*

- *"Bind and remove any negative beings who are in-*

volved with or interfering with this circumstance. Take them to their own right place for healing and transformation in the light."

- *"Clear and heal through all time and space, through all dimensional and parallel realities and universes."*

- *"Clear and transmute all Karma connected to this situation to the limit allowed by Divine law and Divine Grace."*

- *"Clear, cleanse and transmute any negative energy surrounding this circumstance."*

- *"Restore the physical, emotional, mental and higher bodies to God's perfect design for health and wholeness."*

6. Call for full safety and protection for all as a result of this work.

   "I call for full safety and protection for all as a result of this work."

7. Give thanks that it is done.

   "Thank you God/Goddess and so it is."

Chapter 23

All for the Highest Good

Blessed one, be at Peace during this time of transition. In the place of perfect Peace within your own sacred heart, you are best serving the planet. If you wish to help the environment, continue to clean up your own emotional garbage. It is the emotional debris that is outpicturing on the planet in so many ugly and destructive ways. Do not be concerned about the physical issues at this time. Continue as you have been doing with recycling, growing a garden, communicating with nature. But first and foremost, clear, cleanse and heal on the emotional and mental level.

This series of books is designed to maximally assist those who are the leaders of human evolution in clearing their own personal "stuff". Because their consciousness affects all life so strongly, all will receive the benefit. It is not any one person's effort that will make the difference; it is the collective will to good that will be pivotal. And there is no need to focus on those who are holding fast to the old paradigm.

The new paradigm is already in place and is gathering momentum. The Divine Design for the New Earth is already in place. The teachers and leaders are already serving in their right places. The transformation will continue to appear "normal," but change is definitely happening all around. Each blade of grass, each tree, bird, fish and mammal is in the process of massive transformation. Yes, there will be many changes.

Yes, it is a time of letting go. Each person who confronts their own patterns and lets go of what no longer serves them in their own ways serves the whole. This process of letting go is expanding in many beautiful ways, and allowing the space for the new Fifth Dimensional templates to integrate easily and gently (relatively speaking) into their consciousness.

We ask you to be very simple. Allow your life to unfold gently in these days. It is time to take on new tasks and new responsibilities. Allow it all to unfold gracefully. All is well.

Regarding new responsibilities, always ask that your higher self be in charge, and that all divine right action might be the clear choice in this and in all things.

Mikaelah's favorite decree suits these times of change very well. Write it down; carry it with you. Repeat it in whatever circumstance seems to call for it.

"Beloved, mighty I Am Presence,

take command of this situation

and bring it to the highest good

for all concerned."

We are complete for today.

Chapter 24

God's Truth

Blessed one, let us begin with a 15 minute meditation.

Spend time just clearing your energy body and aligning with Truth, with Peace, with Love. It would be wise to repeat this regularly.

⚩

What is truth? There are so many who like to think that they are "only telling the truth" when they spew forth anger, resentment, annoyance, disappointment and judgment.

We would like to direct your attention to the concept that God's Truth of each one's perfection looks quite different from these lesser understandings. When you hold God's Truth for a given situation or any individual or group, then you are holding the Immaculate Concept for that person, group, organization, place or thing. When this level of truth is expressed, a level of soul recognition occurs, and it is possible for great healing to be accomplished.

When I healed, I saw the soul as perfect, whole and complete as God intended. There was never any doubt in my mind that this was the Divine Intention for perfect health for any given individual.

This Truth transcended karmic lessons, and the variety of ways in which humans have learned to draw harm to themselves. Thus, Divine Grace superseded lesser considerations. In your own healing for yourself or with another, know that God's intention is for the perfect expression of health and wholeness. Let there be no doubt in your mind that this person can have that in an instant.

At the very least, see that this being seeking wholeness is set on the path in which every circumstance will converge, to offer exactly what is needed for this to be accomplished. See every block and impediment to perfect health dissolve.

Chapter 25

The Glory of God

Blessed Children of the Light, Be at Peace in the Oneness and the Glory of God the Father, Goddess the Mother, the Holy Trinity of Love, Light and Power, the Eternal radiant glory of God/Goddess/All that Is.

We ask that you sit in the radiance of the Glory of God for a short while. Bathe in the Light and the Love that is God's Will for Good for all life on Earth. We ask that each of you be an anchor – a tuning fork – for these energies. It is through your embodiment of Love, Wisdom and Power that Divine Will for Good expresses on Earth.

Do you sometimes make mistakes? Even when there is error, God can use that for the greater good. It is your intention that is the first directing force, which creates a new path of Light which others can follow. And each one who follows brings their own unique intention and creativity to add to the flow, which creates first a path, then a road, then a vast superhighway of goodness, right action, love in form, light transformed to matter.

Where would you like to see healing directed today? Do you desire greater love and health directed to those who are suffering and in pain? Do you desire the resources of food, shelter and education distributed more widely across the Earth? Do you desire Earth herself to be honored, loved and protected? Do you desire that those who hold a vision of serving the highest good for all now work in harmony and peace to govern?

So many of you have awakened on Earth and see so many needs. Your hearts have opened to give and receive love in ever greater measure. We ask you to place your attention on the good, on the beautiful and on the uplifting. Do not allow your energies to focus on what you do not wish to see perpetuated. Rather, hold a vision for the good that is emerging and growing across the planet. See dedicated men, women and children making a difference around the world. See each one being inspired to bring their gifts and talents to each day make a difference.

Everyone on Earth is unique and carries the potential for an important contribution for the whole. Hold this vision for all life. Give thanks for the good that already exists and the potential good that is daily emerging and growing across the planet. Your attention and intention make a difference.

Choose to serve by continually directing your focus to see the good emerging and expanding. In this way, error diminishes and light expands. Let it be your first step each day.

Chapter 26

See the Good in All things

Blessed child of Light, be at Peace in this time of transformation. Know that all is well. Know that God is here – with you, in you, through you always – all ways.

Do you wish to be a help to others? Shine your light. Share your gifts. Let go of all desire for reward or recognition. It is God in Thee that doeth the works. Be a pure vessel. Allow that which is needful to be directed toward you and from you.

Regarding receiving money for your work: have no attachment to money, but neither do you need to reject it. Let it be a symbol of value for you, but only in the most general way. A widow's mite is of greater proportional value than a millionaire's gold piece. Do not allow the human mind to judge in these circumstances.

Money as a vehicle for the human exchange of goods and services will not last long into this millennium. Soon the delight of giving and receiving of the gifts that have been given will be the true reward. Soon each man, woman and child will be absorbed in their true work, the expression of their Divine gifts and their alignment with right action in each and every now moment.

Imagine that you can have a glimpse of this future, where true delight in life is expressed daily in all things. One where love is shared, hearts are open, blessings abound, and miracles occur in many and delightful ways.

Imagine a world where all needs are met, healing has

already been accomplished, life purposes are fulfilled daily, potential is explored, goodness, beauty and joy are the daily norm.

Oh, yes, this is already happening and it is daily expanding for each life on Earth.

What is the lesson to be shared today, you might ask? The lesson is that life is good, and it keeps on getting better. See the good that is intrinsic in all things. Focus not on what is wrong, but on what is right, and see it expanding. When there is too much focus on what is wrong, on lack, or sadness or dis-ease, it might seem that things will never be made right.

And yet, that is not the lesson of these times. The lesson is that each day, each moment, good is coming to each person. Let the lesson be that it is time now to expand your heart, expand your mind, expand your beliefs to make room for the good that is flowing toward you – and from you – in ever greater measure. And, yes, you need to let go of the past, let go of the pain, the contractions and the fears, so that the restriction and limitation might be reversed. And, yes again, the *Violet Flame* is a wonderful and exquisite tool to transform and transmute the distortions of the past.

But remember a rainbow has many colors. Each color represents God's gifts to all life in all their diversity. Perhaps it is through the pink ray of love that your greatest expansion will occur, or through the golden yellow of wisdom, or the emerald green of science and healing, or the green growth of nature. Perhaps it is through a kitten's exuberance or a snail's small path through your garden. Perhaps it is all of these things.

The greatest lesson is that life is good. That you are good. That God/good expresses in and through you and all life. That God/good expresses uniquely in each person, each culture, each rock, insect and star. Open your heart and mind and see and feel this good that surrounds you. Breathe it in. Know your own body temple to be a hologram of the greatness of All that Is. Every star, every flower, every thought, and word and action is a resonant part of you. And each individual uniquely expresses and grows in wisdom, love and power.

You are a miracle.

Each individual is a miracle of God expression. You are a miracle. Know and love yourself for the miracle of good that you are.

We are complete for today.

Chapter 27

You Are All Healers

Blessed Ones, you are all healers. Your bodies are designed to be self-healing, self-perpetuating. When you began to explore that which is unreal, you began to undo some of your basic programming. Your actual encodements for perfection are embedded in your DNA.

In order to explore dis-ease and death, the actual encodements sometimes had to be changed.

Let us now upgrade and restore your DNA to its original perfection. Your DNA, as it is presently known, is merely that which can be observed with the physical tools of the Third Dimension. The twelve-strand DNA, of which you may have heard, exists primarily on the higher dimensional fields of consciousness and being, and is your Divine template on the Fourth through the Twelfth Dimensions as well.

Exercise 3: 27-1 **Healing Your DNA**

*We will use the **Miracle Wand** for this exercise. Call your Miracle Wand into your dominant hand. Turn on its activation switch. Call in the Angels of Miracles to assist with this next activity. Invite and invoke your full alignment with your I Am Presence, your God Self. Call it thusly.*

Beloved I Am, Beloved I Am, Beloved I Am.

I Am One in Thee. Thou art One in me.

In this Oneness, I am conscious in all levels of being.

I have the power and authority

for all Divinely-aligned right action.

In this Oneness, I Am worthy of all gifts and graces.

Please guide and assist in all I think and say and do,

Especially in this work today.

*(This next step is more fully explained in the book **"Medical Assistance Program (MAP) of the Great White Brotherhood"** by Machaele Small Wright.)*

Ask your I Am Presence to join in the call for the assistance of the overlighting Angel of Healing and the God Pan, who rules the elemental kingdom and the elementals that work with and for your physical body. You will not need to call on your personal MAP team, for this next step in reclaiming your perfect form and perfect function of physical, emotional and mental health.

Set your intention and say:

"In full alignment with my own mighty I Am Presence and all Life, I now command and claim the restoration to full and perfect health in all levels of my RNA-DNA system."

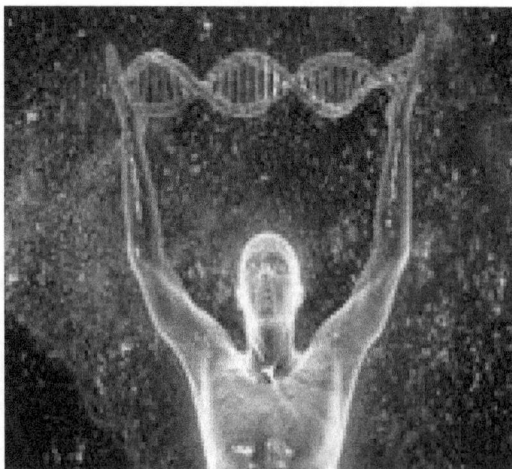

182

Now envision a large replica of the DNA molecule in the space before you.

Take the wand, and carefully draw it from end to end following the spiral. Then reverse the direction. You might notice that the spiral seems to extend infinitely. It is only necessary to work on the defined space. The infinite is already perfect.

Now, again move the wand back and forth on the field outside the DNA hologrammatic image. No spiraling is necessary. This creates a field of protection and safety for both this time of healing and afterwards, to hold the pattern of perfect health in place. Now take the wand and tap the entire field three times. This clears any karma, life lessons, curses, contracts, vows or other agreements that allowed any distortion(s) to occur.

And finally, tap yourself on the crown chakra (top of the head) three times to fully integrate this correction into the four lower bodies (physical, emotional, mental and etheric).

Thank the Angels who have given their assistance. Thank the elementals and especially Pan, for their attention on this activity, and for all their assistance throughout your life. Thank your God Self for the love and protection that is always with you. Thank any other Beings of Light and Love who have offered their time, their attention and their assistance today.

And this is complete.

Chapter 28

The Present Moment

Blessed One, spend a few moments in silent meditation, and we will proceed.

Regrets are time wasters. If you wish to meditate on how to accomplish something faster or better, then look at the available options. Trying to second guess how you might have done something differently in the past can only have value for a present decision. Trying to guess what might be necessary in some potential future does not serve you. There are too many variables that might come into play later. Rather, bless your choices and the reasons for those choices from the past. Call on the *Violet Flame* to purify and transmute any negativity from those choices, AND LET IT GO!

To maximally serve in the present, you must be in the present and bring all of your energy and attention into the present. So let us spend our time today bringing your whole self fully into present time.

Exercise 3: 27-1: **Coming Fully into Present Time**

*Start with **grounding** yourself. Invoke a column of light **(Tube of Light)** from Source to flow down through your head, your spinal column, and through the body, through the crust of the Earth, through all deeper and deeper layers into the core of the Earth. Call on any and all aspects or fragments of yourself not in present time to be tapped with the **Present Time Wand** and brought back to you whole, cleansed and complete.*

*Stand for a moment in a **Pillar of Violet Fire** and allow all that you are to be touched and healed with the qualities of forgiveness and transmutation of all negativity. Forgive yourself and all others, until you know and remember that there is really nothing to forgive.*

Now, step forward into a Pillar of Celestial Blue energy, and allow yourself to be realigned in purpose and divine clarity. And step again into a pillar of Aquamarine Flame, and bathe in the divine qualities which clear, cleanse and heal on all levels of your consciousness.

Sep again into a Pillar of Celestial Rose Pink Flame; bathe in the universal love energies that flow unceasingly from Source into and through all levels of being. Allow every cell and atom of your being to be bathed in Love, as you are renewed and realigned with the perfection that love created you to be.

And again step forward into a Pillar of Golden Yellow Flame. Allow Divine Wisdom to gently correct any misunderstandings you might have ever thought were truth about yourself, your life, the world, creation, All That Is, and the nature of God/Goddess. Know that this Truth, this Wisdom will become more and more available to you as you integrate it and as you need it.

And finally, step into a Pillar of Diamond White Light. Let the energies of purity, of perfection, of infinitely expanding wonder and glory shine in you, around you, through you. Allow your body and soul to be lifted gently and effortlessly to your next right level of being.

*Ask your **Higher Self** and the angels to assist you to release all that no longer serves you at this new level. Call the **Violet Flame** to completely transmute any energy that you are releasing, and let it go.*

And now, allow the Love Light that is God in you to extend from your heart to connect with those you now know and love. Let this light extend to those who will be coming to you to meet and work with at this next level of being. Let this light extend to surround the planet and touch all life. And join with the planet and all life thereon, and extend this light to the whole of creation.

We are complete.

Chapter 29

Blessings

Be at Peace today and all days. We speak to you from the realms of Illumined Peace.

We are the Elohim of Peace and Grace.

Exercise 3: 28-1: **Blessings of Peace and Grace**

Take a moment now to bathe in the Peace and Grace of Eternal Love. Feel waves of Love pouring over you. Know that you are eternally held in the arms of Love. Know that Peace and Grace and Love surround you and fill you. Breathe in the Peace. Breathe in the Grace. Breathe in the Love.

Let all subtle fears dissolve now. Let all worries and doubts dissolve now. You are that Peace. You are that Grace. You are that Love. Separation is an illusion. Worries, doubts and fears are the ties that bind you within the illusion. Let them go, and ask now that all the places in your subtle bodies that have allowed them entry now be healed and restored to Peace and Truth and Love.

Chapter 30

Clearing Your Space

Blessed One, all is well. For today, there is still much that has come up to be dealt with. Spend a short while in meditation and then we will proceed.

Now you see that there are any number of issues still sitting on your mind that are not completed and that cause you ongoing concern. Issues of debt, of apology, of incomplete projects, of new things to do which besiege you daily.

In order for you to be as completely clear, as you wish, to hear me and transcribe in the complexity and purity that you desire, these must be cleared. AND each of these examples are mere metaphors for a larger issue of accumulated "stuff".

Focus on the ongoing accumulation of projects on your desk. This represents a clearing of effluvia that are on your mind, not just your desk. So today, we will be working on "clearing the slate" of projects that are to be discarded, to be placed in a queue, or to be placed on a current "to do" list.

You will be so much happier when you are not constantly trying to review all these things and can get on with those things that are of importance to you now.

Exercise 3:29-1: **Priorities and Letting Go**

Imagine you desk and know that this is a metaphor for your mind. So we will address your mind and the mental constructs that are now ready to be released. First, ask an angel to come to you and sort through all the complexity and rearrange all into three piles.

1 – Things to be let go of.

2 – Things to deal with later.

3 – Things to deal with today.

*You could just take the entire pile of things to let go of and dump them in the **Violet Flame**. But first, let us tap that pile with the **Present Time Wand,** and release the energy that is stuck in the past that has kept them rotating through your mind and across your desk.*

*Now, tap them with the **Miracle Wand** to release any negative energies that might have been connected. This will clear any curses, thought forms or false beliefs, and any judgments you might have ever made against another or against yourself.*

Now, let us imagine that you have been going to school and the classes are over. All notes from those classes are no longer needed and can be discarded. You can let go of all projects that you have been holding on to that might lead to results later. Create a To Do journal. Keep track of what you desire to accomplish and what has been completed. If you need written information, print it out. Use any needed software.

A computer system will allow you the most flexibility in selecting and moving those things from one section to another.

Spend time each day on those things that you truly want to do – things that have value to you and that you believe have value to others. This is what will give you the most encouragement.

*Rome wasn't built in a day. It isn't necessary to do everything at once. A bit every day is more than sufficient. We are complete for today, but in closing let us remind you to cleanse and transmute with **Violet Flame** all that you are releasing.*

Blessings to you. We are the Sacred Heart Flame of Jesus and Mary working with you on the healing of humanity.

Chapter 31

Clearing Negative Influences

Let us share today's lesson on clearing all negative influences from your field.

First, let us notice that there are many ways in which the light body can be affected by negative influences coming from the environment.

Perhaps the negativity is embedded in a book, game, video or movie. Perhaps in attempting to help another, you are attacked subtly, or not so subtly. Have you collected a linked curse? That is, have you attempted to clear a curse from another and picked up a curse or entity yourself because of it? Have you been slimed, or taken on another's false belief, guilt, or shame? Sometimes, there is lingering karma with another waiting to be cleared. Whatever the problem, the solutions are simple.

Each morning set a firm *Tube of Light, Love and Protection* around yourself.

Each time you are in a public setting, place a field of cosmic white light protection around yourself, and ask that a team of protection angels be assigned to keep you clear of all negative influences.

Placing etheric white roses in front, behind, to the left and the right, above and below you both as protection and a signal if something is not right can be extremely helpful. Check regularly to see if they are damaged or discolored. If so, remove and call for *Violet Flame* to transmute the negative energy and replace the rose. Notice if the problem is coming from a particular person, place or situation. Make some decisions about how best to deal with this in the future.

Check your grounding cord daily and after a physical or emotional upset, such as a fall, injury, major argument or shock of any sort.

Set your intention for protection, health, and the highest good for yourself and all concerned, before you begin to work on another.

Each time you give assistance to another, clear your field with the *Violet Flame,* and ask that all negative influences be identified and dealt with appropriately, so that your field remains inviolate. Purify and return all personal energy to the other when you are complete. Call back your own personal energy, purified and cleansed. ASK if there is anything further to be dealt with before you close a session.

Set your intention that there be no repercussions for anyone, due to the work that is done.

Clear your field of any cords or inappropriate connections at the end of a session.

Daily, clear any energy that is not your own, especially emotional energy which tends to collect in the second chakra. Send it into a *Violet Flame* campfire (visualize this) to be thoroughly cleansed before it returns. And immediately refill the space it occupied with White or Gold Light.

At the end of each day, do a complete and thorough cleansing of all that you might have picked up during the day.

• Repeat the Lord's Prayer.

• Use an etheric *Golden Comb* regularly to cleanse the aura. This etheric tool will allow you to notice how your energy field is doing and whether you might have picked up something that is harmful. You might find your aura with holes or tears. You might find gunk or debris embedded in your field. Angels can be asked to help with any corrections needed.

- Cleanse yourself within and throughout the aura by standing in a pillar of *Violet Flame.*
- Refill yourself with Gold and/or White Light.

Before you choose to bring something into your field, whether it is a book, an item at a yard sale, new clothes or car, a new acquaintance or job, or any activity, check your inner guidance if it is for the highest good to proceed.

Regarding influences one might pick up from verbal negativity spouted by another, discord, disharmony, distortion or ugliness seen on the internet or TV or via the written word, always treat with the *Violet Flame,* both for yourself and any others who might be affected. Call in the angels to clear, cleanse and heal as is needed. And ask that blessings to assist those who are perpetrating the negativity might receive the help they need, to find their own healing and to cease polluting the atmosphere. Ask if there is anything further you are to do. Then let it go completely.

Beloved St. Germain and Angels of the Violet Flame,
Blaze Violet Flame in, through, and around this situation.
Bring forgiveness, transmute all negativity,
And restore Divine Freedom to all concerned.

For specific higher order assistance, call on Jesus, Quan Yin, Saint Germain, Lord Melchizedek, Archangel Lord Metatron, Goddess Sekhmet, for large difficult cases, or Commander Ashtar for negative extraterrestrials and their implants, tracking or recording devices, ships, underground bases, etc. Assistance can be requested from the Great Central Sun. Negativity can be sent to the Cosmic Void for recycling into the infinite unmanifest. Prior to this last step, check that it is for the highest good, or if there is another preferable step.

Your Prayer Request:

"I call on Jesus the Christ, Jesus the Christ, Jesus the Christ.

"Please come and give me maximum assistance allowed by law

"To clear, cleanse and heal myself and all involved in this situation.

"Especially, ………."

. . . . .

"Fill me with Divine Love, Wisdom, Harmony, Peace and Joy."

"Archangel Michael, Archangel Michael, Archangel Michael,

"Please bring your Blue Flame Angels to guard and protect me."

. . . . .

"Bind and remove any negative beings, and bring them to their own right place for healing and transformation in the light.

"Fill my field with white and gold light."

. . . . .

"Commander Ashtar, leader of the Galactic Federation fleet of starships, workng to serve the White Light of the Christ and the Will of Mother / Father God,

"Please remove any implants, devices, trackers, tracers or other implements that are not for my highest good. Remove any cords or other connections, and burn them back to their source. Neutralize the source, and remove any extraterrestrial beings, ships, or fleets. Clear any related underground bases. Send all beings related to these to their own right place for healing and transformation in the Light."

. . . . .

"Remove every record, memory, pattern and trace of these influences from every cell and atom of my being, from all dimensional and interdimensional realities, all times – past, present and future, and all parallel or alternate universes or realities."

"Thank you God it is so done right now and forever."

. . . . .

For clearing karma between yourself and another when you feel a lot of discordant energy or negativity between you, you might use the **Ho'o Ponopono Prayer.**

I'm sorry.
Please forgive me.
I love you.
Thank you.
I release it.

Repeat several times if necessary.

This simple prayer can be extremely useful before meeting a new person or prior to a job interview. It is also extremely helpful to clear any unidentified karma when there is a group gathering.

Chapter 32

The Enemy of Innocence

It was during a final edit of this book that a significant issue emerged and thus demanded something more be added. A dream brought it to my (Mikaelah's) attention. And with Jesus' permission and encouragement this next section is now included.

I, Jesus, will now continue as we address an extremely important topic. I say we because Mikaelah and I work as a team in the co-creation of this book. What attracted her attention was the presence of an indwelling "saboteur." This being was as well-hidden as any enemy spy. Its mission was to insidiously undermine her self-confidence and, as well, insert error whenever possible. In this case, it was a single word that held a negative emotional charge for her and for all who might read it.

She has willingly revealed her deepest issues herein, so that all who are choosing to cleanse at their own deepest levels might be given this sacred assistance.

She has done quite a bit of work with a process called Alchemical Hypnotherapy®. Within this teaching are a variety of tools to examine and heal the inner landscape of beliefs, memories, subpersonalities, and to connect with the presence of the Higher Self in many guises[11].

---

11 *There is more about the work with the inner sub-personalities in Mikaelah's first book "Live in Love - A Life Handbook for the New Golden Age" in Chapter 19, Sacred Relationships. To explore more about the teachings of Alchemical Hypnotherapy, go to* www.AlchemyInstitute.com

Here one can explore the influences of the Inner Child, the Inner Judge, the Inner Skeptic and many more parts of the subconscious self, which can be identified, re-educated and raised to new levels of consciousness, thereby creating conscious allies, rather than unconscious parts that resist your highest aspirations.

As well, there are also often hidden presences which are not a true part of the inner landscape. We might call this a saboteur, especially when it is well-disguised and hidden for many years. It does not belong. It is not about re-educating and raising its consciousness. It needs to be identified and cast out.

Such beings have only your harm in mind. True sub-personalities might be misguided, but they are trying to help.

To identify and heal if such is present, we refer you to Chapters 6 and 31, or suggest you find a spiritual professional who is qualified in identifying, clearing and healing Inner Plane issues with negative beings.

Author's note: Well, I must admit, working with this book has changed me. I feel as though it is all right to add my own thoughts and feelings to what is presented from Jesus. I recognize that my own very real, very human emotions, are a part of what is being worked with, and serve as a pertinent example of the ways in which healing proceeds.

Shortly after I/we added this chapter, I awoke to hear a song, which was also an introduction to the Presence that was with me and was filling me with light. The song was: "Mighty Astrea, Blessed Elohim" - a hymn to one of the Elohim. I sat for a while, bathing in this light and then I thought perhaps she might have a message to share. This is what I received.

Dear One, I Am with you now, in this pure and immaculate Now, blessed by purifying, cooling, soothing rain.

I Am with you.

Let us speak of the Great I Am that I Am. I Am in me, I Am in Thee. God in All Her Grace and Glory. Who is God? What is God?

God is all that you see. All that you know. All that is on every level, every dimension – the seen and unseen, the known and unknown, the created and that which is potential.

Blessed One, you have been watching videos: near death visits to heaven and hell; children born and growing with terrible disfigurements and then turning to the more uplifting, listening to my song "Mighty Astrea" and calling for Miracles of healing and restoration.

You are concerned that somehow writing about and exploring the nature of what is not real, and even how to clear and heal it – that somehow the very act of dwelling on negativity makes the very contamination you seek to expunge/delete.

Well, dear one, it is not so. Closing your eyes to error does not make it go away. Rather, shining the Light and Love of God allows the Real to be revealed and the unreal to be healed.

But see with the Eyes of God. Let God's Plan for restoring each to their own perfection be your intention. Join your will with God's Will – seeing and knowing that all works for the greater good.

The Earth and all life are in the midst of major transformation. That which is unreal is coming to global attention. Not so you can wallow in anger or despair. Rather, so you can shine the Light of God on it and let it be corrected.

Dear One, we urge you to pray each day that God's Miracles of Grace be made manifest in every situation where there is pain and suffering or disease. Call the angels to intervene in every circumstance. Stories of miracles abound. Let yourself be the instrument that calls for health and wholeness. Hold the image of God/good in your mind no matter what need you observe around you.

And remember – "There is no order of difficulty in a miracle."[12]

---

12 Lesson from the book "A Course in Miracles."

Chapter 33

True Innocence

Beloved Child of the Most High, Be at Peace. For this book and all the chapters are part of the teachings of the innermost levels of *the Tao*. And one must be centered in Love, in Peace, in order to successfully receive the messages.

Dearest child of light, always allow yourself to know that state of being of the innocent child. Purity, Truth and Love are your true nature. All the judgments, distortions and false beliefs are not real. Spend a moment right now and give your angels full permission to fully clear, cleanse and heal all levels of consciousness that have ever held these errors.

Exercise 3: 33-1: **Restoration of Original Innocence**

*Stand in a pillar of White Christed Light. Let yourself be fully purified and restored to Divine Innocence and Divine Purity. There may be places in your physical, emotional, mental and etheric bodies where records of being judged, punished, beaten or killed still hold a charge from the pain of those experiences. Tap them with the **Present Time Wand**. Now take the 7th dimensional **Miracle Wand** and stand fully united with your **I Am Presence** and tap body, emotions, mind and soul.*

*Now, walk with your Higher Self into the **Hall of Records** and review your own records. Tap those with the **Miracle Wand** and see any stains and damage fully, completely and eternally cleansed.*

Know that you have fully released these errors, and see yourself restored to your perfection.

And now ask your Higher Self to assist you to fully clear, cleanse and heal any curses or negatively charged statements of any kind sent by you to others. Fully release every record, memory, pattern and trace from yourself and any others you have affected, from all the effects of any and all condemnations and errors of judgment and false beliefs in all times, all dimensions, all realities. Ask and intend that only Divine Will, Divine Wisdom and Divine Judgment hold sway in all circumstances, past, present and future.

Allow yourself all the time you need to complete this section. It is not designed to be quickly read and forgotten. This is not a race but a journey. Each step must have its own time and attention to be completed. These written steps are just the entryway to a larger, fuller experience, guided by your teachers, guides, angels and ***Higher Self***.

And there is one more step to be taken before we are complete today.

Allow yourself to breathe and to smile, dear ones. Allow yourself to believe that it is possible to correct the errors of the ages with these few, simple steps. Let all external habits and patterns that have been tied to these false beliefs about your unworthiness now be fully and completely released as well. See and know your own true beauty. Know the love that you are and allow it to shine out through your eyes, through your smile, through your very skin and bones. Know that you are fully and completely whole now and forever.

And we are complete with this chapter
and this book.

200

Appendices

Glossary of Terms

Ascended Master:

Ascended Masters are believed to be individuals who have lived in physical bodies, acquired the Wisdom and Mastery needed to become Immortal and Free of the cycles of "re-embodiment" and karma, have attained their "Ascension" (the Sixth Initiation), and have regained full union with his/her "Mighty I AM Presence." (Wikipedia)

Jesus is said to have created a Divine Template or Blueprint for the Initiation and Ascension process for humanity through the example of His life.

Ascension: The specific Spiritual Initiation in which an individual or group is raised in consciousness into union with the I Am Presence. There are levels upon levels of Ascension into greater and greater union with the individuality of God called I AM.[13]

Wikipedia adds this: "The Ascended Master Teachings refer to the Sixth Initiation as Ascension."

At one time, it was believed that one died or left the planet following the Ascension and served from the inner planes. Due to shifts in the planetary field, human readiness and planetary need, it is now considered not uncommon for individuals to take various levels of Ascension and remain to

---

13 See Chapter 10, "Initiations - Human and Solar" in Mikaelah Cordeo's book *Live in Love - A Life Handbook for the New Golden Age* for more details on levels of consciousness, Initiation, and Ascension. Also explore the Internet for more extensive definitions, discussions and points of view from various groups, especially: Summit Lighthouse, Saint Germain Foundation, the Hearts Center, and Radiant Rose Academy.

serve as an embodiment of their I Am Presence on Earth. Indeed, it is the Divine Plan that this be so.

Ascension Rosary Prayer:

> Hail Mary, full of Grace,
> The Lord is with Thee.
> Blessed art Thou among women, and
> Blessed is the Fruit of ThyWomb, Jesus.
>
> Holy Mary, Mother of us all,
> Blend with us, children of the Sun/Son
> For we have consciously won our Ascension.
> Right now and forevermore, I AM!
>
> *Stanza 1 is the traditional Rosary given to St. Domnic in 1203.*
> *Stanza 2 was received by Mary Clarice McChrist in 1976 and updated in*
> *1993 and 2002.*

Chohans: Certain Ascended Masters are known as Chohans, or the primary planetary teachers, of the spiritual Rays which hold certian distinct Divine energies such as love, wisdom, health, peace, etc. Saint Germain and El Morya Kahn are among the best known of the Chohans.

Decree: A formal prayer, often repeated or sung, which consists of three steps. 1) Calling on specific Divine Beings to bless and hold a sacred field for the prayer to follow; 2) the prayer itself which is usually rhythmic and/or rhyming and states the desired outcome in the most positive and uplifting manner possible; 3) a closing or sealing action.

Decrees are often chanted with increasing speed to increase the vibrational frequency and power. That and repetition increase the momentum of the prayer.

Divine Blueprint: A 5th dimensional grid structure that sets the Divine Design or Blueprint for an individual, group or planet.

Field of Oneness or Unified Field: During an experimental project in Mount Shasta, California, creating a new template for the planetary Councils of Light[14], we discovered a meditation process that anchored the unified field in our individual grid structures. This was a step in the larger process of achieving a Oneness consciousness at the planetary level.

From a place of individual unification with the I Am Presence, it is possible to then connect at a group level with a group I Am Presence and to then experience a unified field at the group level. Ultimately, such groups, will link with Higher Dimensional Councils of Light and express the next level of the Divine Plan at a group level.

In the *Starseed Transmission*, author Ken Carey introduced the concept of a new level of unified consciousness to be held by all humanity as we explore the universe following the transformation process now underway on Earth.

Four Lower Bodies: This term refers to the Physical, Emotional, Mental and Etheric energy bodies of a human being.

Gold Comb: An etheric tool to clear and tidy your aura. Imagine fine threads or hairs all over your aura and use the comb to straighten. If there is major damage ask your I Am Presence for assistance and use other tools as needed. Using it lets you see how your aura is doing.

Grounding Cord: Grounding is an energy technique that allows one to be fully in present time. One may visualize a cord from the base of the spine down into the center of the Earth or from the chakras in the soles of the feet into the Earth. One can imagine roots like a tree leaving you connected and centered.

---

14 Go to www.counciloflight.4t.com for more information and the specific Unified Field meditation.

Hall of Records: Here referring to an etheric location also known as the Akashic Records. These records are a compendium of thoughts, events, and lifetimes of all individuals encoded in a non-physical plane of existence. Here soul records can be explored and healed.

Higher Self: That aspect of you which resides in the higher (heavenly) realms beyond the four lower bodies. The first of these levels is that of Christ consciousness. Contact with the Higher Self offers truth, guidance, healing, joy, love and spiritual replenishment. At this time, aspects of the Higher Self and I Am Presence are merging with the human personal self in the glorious expression of the Divine Plan. This means that a new level of the Higher Self takes over the role of overseeing one's spiritual progress, guidance and development.

Ho'o Ponopono Prayer: This concept was introduced to many through a story about a Psychiatrist in a Hawaiian hospital for the criminally insane. To be brief, he used the prayer for each inmate daily and in so doing, healed issues of staff turnover and discontent, and ultimately each patient became so much better that the hospital was closed because it was no longer needed. There are many stories on the internet. Many individuals and groups are using it regularly for healing.

It is incredibly useful to clear karmic issues with anyone you meet. It can be used particularly when a new group comes together, so that each person can quickly clear any lingering karma with one another. (see also p. 136)

Hum Sa Mantra: It is taught by certain Indian gurus that the sound of the in-breath, *Hum*, and the sound of the out-breath, *Sa*, can be repeated consciously as the mantra "*Hum Sa*" – translated as "I Am That" – the name of God. Thus, one is always speaking the name of God unconsciously with each breath. Working with this mantra consciously helps to anchor the I Am Presence in the physical form and is a useful tool both pre- and post- Ascension.

I Am Presence: That aspect of the Higher Self which represent the levels beyond the Holy Christ Self at the Fifth Dimension. The Individual Divine Self is always in union with God/Goddess/All that Is. Thus, when Jeus said, "I and the Father are One," he reflected his union on this level. One could also claim, "I and the Mother are One."

Initiation: A spiritual step which enables one to achieve a new level of consicousness. An individual or a group opens to greater levels of love and wisdom and raises all bodies to a higher vibratory rate. One step of this path includes the Ascension or direct union with the I Am Presence.

Present Time Wand: This inner plane, energy tool was introduced by Arian Sarris in her books *Healing Your Past* and *Heart Wisdom*. One can imagine receiving a 5th dimensional wand which has the power to release energy stuck in the past (including experiences from infancy, childhood, and even adult events that have strong emotional charge, as well as past life experiences or traumas that need to be cleared). This allows you to be more fully in the present time which is now merging into the fifth dimension.

You use it by imagining it in your hand, and tapping your physical body, chakras or auric field where there is stuck energy (emotionally charged memory that keeps recurring and draws you into the past.) A burst of light is released and there is near instantaneous clearing as energy is freed up for your use in present tine. This can be used in conjunction with Violet Flame and other healing/ transmutation tools.

Sacred Merkaba: Three words are the basis of the word Merkaba. Mer means light. Ka is from the Egyptian which means spirit and Ba another Egyptian word means character or personality - thus the individual part of a soul.

Merkaba as a shape is created of Divine Geometry - two star tetrahedrons - and used as an energy vehicle to transport spirit /soul to alternate realities and dimensions.

Saint Germain: It was the Ascended Master St. Germain who introduced many sacred teachings to Guy Ballard in the early 1930's when he lived and worked near Mt. Shasta, California. Most significant were those relating to the I Am Presence, personal and planetary Ascension, and the Violet Flame. These teachings explained many formerly secret teachings and are the foundational spiritual understanding for many who are rather loosely called New Agers around the world.

Soul Templates: These are higher dimensional overlays and can include personality structures, levels of wealth intended for a given lifetime, success in relationships, health strengths or challenges, certain DNA patterns, hereditary or family/social patterns for learning, and timing for various spiritual, mental, emotional and physical growth experiences.

Sword of Truth of Archangel Michael: This etheric sword is your gift to use for good. You can cut attaching cords, identify those who do not serve the light, and use it to cast a field or tube of light and protection around yourself.

Look for video link for receiving your own sword from Archangel Michael and ways to use it on www.cordeobooks.wordpress.com

Template: An etheric grid structure that sets the Divine Design for an individual. Templates can include personality structures, levels of wealth intended for a given lifetime, success in relationships, health strengths or challenges, DNA patterns, hereditary or family/social patterns for learning, and timing for various spiritual, mental, emotional and physical growth experiences.

Tube of Light: A field of protection that can and should be invoked daily through decrees, prayers and silent meditation. One can visualize a tube of white light that extends infinitely upward and down into the center of the Earth, extending out about three feet in all directions around the body. Additional levels of protectin can be used that call for the Blue Flame of protection and the Violet Flame of Transmutaiton. Many variations have been developed and might be found through a diligent search of the internet.

Seven Sacred Flames or Rays:

Each color in the visible spectrum holds a different frequency or vibration. As an activity of light, it is also considered to be encoded with sacred meaning and Divine qualities. Archangels and angels are uniquely linked to one or the other of the rays. On Earth, there are certain Ascended Master teachers who are designated as the primary teacher or Chohan of a particular ray. For more information about the Seven main planetary rays and the five hidden rays, explore Mikaelah's book, *Live in Love,* chapters 7 and 8, the internet links in the appendix or do an internet search. The book website **www.cordeobooks.wordpress.com** also offers live links.

Blue Flame: The color blue is associated with the 1st Ray and its qualities are Faith, trust and Divine Will. The Archangels are Michael and Faith. Lord El Morya Kahn is the Chohan.

Pink Flame: Is 2nd Ray energy of Love. The Archangels are Chamuel and Charity. The Chohan is Paul the Venetian.

Yellow Flame: Third Ray energy is Wisdom and Divine Intelligence. The Archangels are Jophiel and Christine. The Chohan is Lord Lanto.

Ascension Flame: The color of this 4th Ray energy is White. The qualities include purity and ascension. The archangels of this ray are Gabriel and Hope. Serapis Bey is the Chohan of this ray.

Green Flame: The 5th Ray brings the energy of healing, science, and wealth. The Archangels are Raphael and Lady Regina (formerly Mother Mary, but she has been reassigned due to her work for the Earth. The Chohan is Lord Hilarion.

Resurrection Flame: The colors of the 6th Ray are described as either Red/Ruby and Gold or Purple and Gold. The qualities of this Divine energy include ministering service and the healing and raising of the body to its highest place of health at its current level of vibration, as a prelude to an ascension/initiatic step into the next level of vibration/consciousness. The archangels are Uriel and Donna Grace. The Chohan is Lady Nada. She embodied as Mary Magdalene during Jesus' lifetime.

Violet Flame: Violet is the highest frequency color of the visible spectrum. Each color (often called flames or rays) also represent different Divine qualities. Violet is a 7th Ray energy which transmutes negativity, imparts freedom and forgiveness, and clears karma. It can be used for individuals, groups, family lineage, national and planetary healing as well as clearing and transmuting solar, galactic and universal issues. Archangels Zadkiel and Holy Amethyst hold this ray. Lord Saint Germain is the Chohan (or planetary teacher) of this ray for Earth.

As these rays or energies come into this universe they are stepped down in intensity from the universal, to the galactic, to the solar and to the planetary levels. Working with rays at the different levels of intensity is sometimes appropriate when larger scale healing is being accomplished.

There is some diversity in the information that has been received by various channels, which is due primarily to the fact that there is so much information that has been heretofore lost or hidden, that it isn't possible to reveal it all at once. Thus, partial understanding might make it seem that there is a disagreement or even that some are right and others are not.

Rather, look for that which is the primary and basic understanding. Trust your own knowing about what is Truth and work with that. Later information will clear up any discrepancies.

As well, there are new rays coming onto the planet and because they are of a higher frequency and more complex in nature, different indivduals might perceive the colors somewhat differently, and one might understand that one quality is expressed and another identify a different one.

Bibliography

Suggested readings for personal growth, healing and spiritual expansion:

Live in Love – A Life Handbook for the New Golden Age by Mikaelah Cordeo

Healing Your Past by Arian Sarris

Heart Wisdom - Channeled Messages from Aruhatala of Telos by Arian Sarris

The Blessed Mother's Blue Rose of the Healing Heart by Mary Clarice McChrist

The Celestine Prophecy - James Redfield

A Course in Miracles - Institute for Inner Peace

The Gnosis and the Law by Tellis S Papastavro

Medical Assistance Program (MAP) of the Great White Brotherhood by Machaelle Small Wright

The Seven Sacred Flames by Aurelia Louise Jones
The Starseed Transmission by Ken Carey

Gratitude Creates Miracles by Christine Savory

Radical Forgiveness by Colin Tipping

For Children:

Gift of the Leprechauns by Mikaelah Cordeo

A Child's Golden Age Handbook by Mary Clarice McChrist

Internet Links

for Mikaelah Cordeo

www.mcordeo.4t.com

www.cordeobooks.wordpress.com

www.mcordeo.wordpress.com

www.counciloflight.4t.com

www.goldenrose.blogspot.com

Other Spiritual Teaching Sites

www.AnOpenDoorofLove.com

www.ariansarris.wordpress.com

www.mother-matrix.com

www,HeartsCenter.org

www.SummitLighthouse.com

www.WalktheEarthasaLivingMaster.com

www.mtshastarising.wordpress.com

Visit **www.MtShastaAuthorsGuild.com**

Explore **Mt Shasta Authors Guild** with
highlights of the spiritual authors and teachers
of Mount Shasta.

Showcasing books, dvds, mp3s, videos,
products and services.

Sign up for our **Authors E-zine.**

Check out the videos of author book talks and more.

If you are plannning to visit Mount Shasta or just want to
find out a little more, explore our **Events page** for local
and internet events available throughout the year for Mount
Shasta. See who is available for telephone consultations or
private and group events in Mount Shasta, as well as who
can bring a presentation to your local area.

Coming 2015-2016:

Mt Shasta Artists Guild

Mt Shasta Musicians Guild

Mt Shasta Practitioners Guild

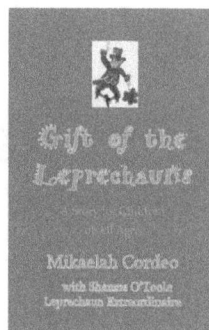

214

Mikaelah Cordeo, Ph.D. is a Channel and Anointed Messenger for Mother/Father God, Angels and Ascended Masters. As an Annointed Messenger she brings through both the words and the energetic blessing of those Beings of Light with whom she works.

Following a successful career in psychology and gerontology and raising three wonderful children, she awakened to the spiritual path in 1984. Mikaelah then followed her life-long dream to know God more deeply and to share spiritual healing, counseling and teaching.

Trained by the Ascended Masters on the Inner Planes, she especially works with Lord Jesus, Mother Mary, Saint Germain, Sanat Kumara and Archangel Michael. She has received unique Divine Empowerments to offer Sacred Initation and Ascension Assistance and "Star Nation Light Body Activations" opening you to new levels of Soul Empowerment and Divine Purpose.

Mikaelah lives and teaches in Mount Shasta, California and offers Ascension gatherings, classes and private sessions. At the request of the Buddha in 2004, she has been offering esoteric Wesak celebrations around the Western United States during the Taurus Full Moon (usually in May) to share the Buddha's blessings from the highest light infusion and download of the Divine Plan for the year.

Mikaelah is now working with a team of Mount Shasta teachers and authors to co-create the *Mount Shasta Authors Guild* as part of the Buddha's **Oneness Initiative** for the Earth as we move into the Fifth Dimension.

To learn more visit her website: **mcordeo.4t.com** and
MountShastaAuthorsGuild.com

Back cover photo: This unposed photo of Mikaelah with Jesus was taken at the "Conclave of the Mother" in 1996, during a sacred dance.

www.ingramcontent.com/pod-product-compliance
Lightning Source LLC
LaVergne TN
LVHW051504080426
835509LV00017B/1906